Counselling on Campus

Counselling on Campus provides insight into the many different reasons why students and young people choose to come for counselling, and demonstrates how counselling enables people to grow emotionally, psychologically and spiritually. This book also explores how counsellors in university campuses and colleges act as a bridge to academic excellence by enabling their clients to develop awareness of their 'feeling' self alongside their intellectual capacity, aspects which can then enhance their whole learning skills.

Fictitious case stories bring each topic to life, exploring the deepest human emotions and grounding advice on best practice firmly in scenarios that readers will encounter in their clinical work. Divided into six distinct parts, the chapters explore:

- Managing change
- Reasons why people seek counselling
- Group work
- Working as a counsellor
- Ethical frameworks for practice
- Professional support.

An essential read for any counsellor or trainee, who is interested in working within a university setting, this book provides readers with a comprehensive understanding of what occurs in the counselling room. It may also be of interest to advisory staff working with students in educational environments and individuals thinking of having counselling themselves.

Maggie Yaxley Smith worked as a humanistic counsellor, marital counsellor, clinical supervisor, Head of a University Counselling Service and group facilitator for more than 35 years. She has written articles and books about counselling and working as a labyrinth facilitator. Today, she writes poetry booklets to raise funds for a local homeless charity.

'Most societies expect young people to readily find their places. Can this really be so easy?

Drawing on her vast experiences as a counsellor, and her long-standing practice on a university campus, Maggie Yaxley Smith sheds light on the many challenges young people face when they leave home.

Building a solid centre within themselves, among these challenges, needs support. Yaxley Smith goes further in stating that true inner power and true inner potential can be gained in working skilfully through trauma in a counselling setting.

This is a wonderful handbook for students, university staff, counsellors and anyone working with young people. It addresses many concerns and offers help through a comprehensive "tool kit" for daily life.

Each case study highlights the importance of counselling on campus. Yaxley Smith emphasises the gravity of counselling in fostering a positive relationship with oneself – especially in the face of bereavement, depression, addiction, neurodiversity, eating disorder, burn-out, domestic violence and more.

Building strength and resilience, and learning to care for oneself, play a significant part in becoming a responsible member of society.'

Agnes Schmitz-Perfect, *Craniosacral therapist, Bach Flower consultant*

Counselling on Campus

A Practical Guide for Mental Health Practitioners Working in Higher and Further Education

Maggie Yaxley Smith

Routledge
Taylor & Francis Group
LONDON AND NEW YORK

Designed cover image: © Getty Images

First published 2027
by Routledge
4 Park Square, Milton Park, Abingdon, Oxon OX14 4RN

and by Routledge
605 Third Avenue, New York, NY 10158

Routledge is an imprint of the Taylor & Francis Group, an informa business

British Library Cataloguing-in-Publication Data
A catalogue record for this book is available from the British Library

ISBN: 9781041274131 (hbk)
ISBN: 9781041274124 (pbk)
ISBN: 9781003754244 (ebk)

DOI: 10.4324/9781003754244

Typeset in Times New Roman
by codeMantra

Contents

Acknowledgements

I would like to thank my husband, Chris, for his many years of encouragement and support – first for my work as a counsellor over many years, and then for his continued support for my various writing projects, including this book. He has always been there for me when I have needed to talk, walk or play.

I would like to thank Patmarie Coleman and Gerard McGill, from whom I gained so much wisdom over the years of working together, for their help and comments on my initial book proposal. I would also like to thank counsellor, David Mortimore, for his more recent, helpful, 'younger views' on my proposal.

My work has been enriched by several wise clinical supervisors, but Brian Graham was the supervisor I worked with most recently and for the longest time, whose 'super-vision' was both enabling and invaluable. I thank him for his many insights and constant support.

I want to thank Lauren Redhead, Editor at Routledge/Taylor & Francis, for making this book happen, with patience, interest and lots of support.

Most of all, I want to thank all the clients, supervisees and colleagues that I have worked with for having the trust and courage to share their experiences, their pain and their vulnerability in order to heal themselves and build truly successful lives for themselves.

About the Author

I worked as a counsellor for 35 years. I initially gained a Certificate in Marriage Guidance Counselling; completed a course in Intermediate Transactional Analysis Psychotherapy; I was accredited with the Association for Student Counselling (now AUCC) in 1987 and 1992. I was accredited and registered as a Senior Practitioner with the British Association for Counselling and Psychotherapy in 1993, 1999, 2004 and up until my retirement in 2011. Also, I was a member of the Association for University and College Counsellors and the Heads of University Counselling Services group. I helped to found the regional Kent Group of Students Counsellors and Catalyst, a local networking group of counsellors and therapists.

For 20 years, I was Head of the University of Kent Counselling Service as well as a supervisor of placements, trainees and qualified counsellors. I facilitated groups on self-esteem, relaxation/meditation, stress awareness, counselling skills, resilience and others for staff and students. I have experience of working as a counsellor for: Relate, a local Women's Refuge, Employment Assistance Programmes, the Prison Service and a private practice, working with a wide selection of clients, including priests and nuns training to be counsellors. I co-facilitated a personal growth group of past and present residents of the Canterbury Women's Refuge. I supervised and supported a group of students trained as Niteline support workers and was on the management committee of Niteline. I facilitated a variety of crisis groups for staff and students following serious incidents and death of a student and facilitated groups for overseas students in fresher's week. I ran courses on Counselling Skills, Stress Awareness, Self-Esteem, Increasing Motivation and Managing Change.

After completing a one-year Diploma in Philosophy, I went on to achieve an MA in 1996, as a part-time student, in Women's Studies with special options in Psychoanalysis, Sexuality and Philosophy and a dissertation on Anthroposophy as a Feminist Philosophy and Education. I successfully completed the first year of an MA in Creative Writing in 2006, but I didn't continue because of increased responsibilities at work. My main interests apart from family and friends are creative writing, yoga, hiking, singing in a community choir and being a member of a meditation group. I belong to a local Canterbury poetry group, 'Save As'.

I was involved in a colleague's project to build a labyrinth on the University of Kent campus and attended a week's training course with Veriditas at Chartres Cathedral to become a labyrinth facilitator and have run groups on the Canterbury campus with staff and students.

Publications

Books

Finding Love in the Looking Glass: A Book of Counselling Case Stories (2014) London, Karnac. (now with Taylor and Francis).

Description

Never has there been such a hunger for relationships – with ourselves and with others. There are valuable insights within these dynamic dialogues between clients and their counsellor. Although the clients are entirely fictitious, they become totally real and easy to connect with as the reader is drawn deeper into the unfolding intimacy of the counselling room. A variety of interventions are used, but what proves most instrumental in empowering clients is the relationship they develop with themselves. These clients show us how we can successfully overcome outdated survival patterns and make effective new choices that work for us. The four topics covered are: **Anorexia**, including issues about cultural identity; **Relationship Breakdown**, including themes about boarding schools, class and cultural differences; **Depression**, including suicidal ideation; **Cocaine Addiction**, stemming from childhood sexual abuse. An introduction explains the structure and professional requirements of a counsellor. A brief outline of the themes precedes each case story, and there is an appendix of useful books, articles and online information. From 35 years of experience as a counsellor, supervisor and Head of a University Counselling Service, the author shows how she has used her particular style of brief counselling to enable and witness this remarkable process. **Chapters in other books:**

Learning Journeys with the Labyrinth and Creating Reflective Space in Higher Education. Part III: Campus and Community, Chapter 16: *Creating a Space for Play: A Counsellor's Perspective*. Palgrave, (May, 2016). A book edited by Professor Bernard Moss and Dr. Jan Sellers. Series editor, Sally Brown.

Counselling Articless

'Four Seasons on Campus', Association for University and College Counsellors Journal (August, 1999).

'Bringing Case Notes Alive', British Association for Counselling and Psychotherapy Journal (June, 2001).

'The Canterbury Labyrinth', AUCC Journal (May, 2010).

'And Now For a Walk in the Park', AUCC Journal (September, 2011).

Tales from the Counselling Room, **Therapy Today** (April, 2015, Volume 26, Issue 3, pp.16–17).

I did have a Counselling Blog: www.counsellingcasestories.wordpress.com but have discontinued it, but it is still online and could be continued.

As Head of the Counselling Service, I produced a variety of self-help leaflets within the counselling service on topics such as Stress Management, Self-Esteem, Assertiveness, Time Management, Homesickness, Using the University Labyrinth, A Fresher's Guide to Thriving and others. Some of them may still be on my blog, and I've included some of these in this book.

Woman's Studies Articles

'Standing on Strong Shoulders', Suffragette Stories (2018). https://sufragettestories.omkeka.net.

Historical Article

'The Tempestuous Birth of Harca', Bob Up And Down (short version) (HARCA, Harbledown and Rough Common Association, September, 2004) (long version) **Harbledown Occasional Papers No.1**. (HARCA, December, 2004).

Poetry Collections

To raise money for 'Catching Lives', a charity that supports homeless people: Bearing Witness (2022) and Homage to Mother Earth (2024) (self-published)

Poems and Songs

Poem: "*The Heart Beats of Harbledown*" in Harbledown Occasional Papers No.2. (HARCA, 2007).

Poem: "*What it Begins With*" in Statement for the Prosecution (in aid of Amnesty International and CND), Categorical Books, (2005).

Poem: *'Purification' in* "Did I Tell You" 131 Poems for Children in Need (2010) *Edited by Nicky Gould and Vicky Wilson published by WordAid.org.uk in 2010*

Poem: '*The Park Bench in Joubert Park*' published in, The New Writer, No 112 (Autumn 2012)

Poem: *'I Watch, I Wait, I Walk'* shortlisted in Canterbury Poet of the Year Competition, 2017.

Lyrics for songs: performed by the Maridadi Singers, two songs, "*An Everyday Carol*" and "*Angel Fest*" performed in Canterbury Cathedral.

Part One

Managing Change

Chapter 1

New Students Managing Change

This chapter is setting the scene for you, beginning a course as a trainee counsellor or therapist, to think about what you want from this training course and what will most support you during this time. It is important for you as a new student to reflect on what skills and experiences you already have to draw upon to get the most out of this course. If you have counselling to help you in this process, think about what you want to achieve from your counselling, as that will most help you develop the understanding, skills and self-awareness you will need to do this work well.

Counselling and therapy training courses are some of the hardest courses to cope with. Trainees are challenged in the very deepest part of their being since the most important tool that they are learning to use is themselves. However, it is important to remember the reasons and excitement that led you to choose to do this work. It is important to trust your intuition and skills and know that you will find the best direction for your creative and intellectual strengths to enable you to make a smooth transition from your training course to becoming an increasingly competent and professional counsellor.

Whether you have already experienced having counselling yourself or not, it is important for you to experience the counselling process firsthand, as you start out on this very rewarding but complex course of study.

What Do You Want from Your Counselling Course?

At the end of this training course, what do you want to feel you have enjoyed and achieved from your course? Is success just about getting a good result, or is it about getting something enlivening and joyful out of the whole experience. Beginning any course is an opportunity to learn so much about your relationship with yourself, about your relationship with your studies and your relationship with other people. You will learn what inspires and interests you and what bores and irritates you. This is an opportunity to discover what skills you have and what skills you want to learn; to discover what kind of counsellor you want to be and what kind of work you are most interested in doing. During your training course, you are becoming part of a community that you can both learn from and contribute to. Finding your place and finding yourself in this space are important lessons for the rest of your life.

DOI: 10.4324/9781003754244-2

For those of you who want to go on to work with university or college students, some of the feelings you are experiencing now are very similar to those feelings your future clients will be feeling.

It is important to normalise difficulties that come up and know that you have the strength, power and intelligence to tackle virtually anything and anyone that comes your way. Allow yourself to ask for help with anything that feels uncomfortable. Allow yourself to make mistakes; they are our best way of learning new skills. You will make good choices and may need to accept **some** less good, but familiar choices, until you can add a new repertoire of possibilities.

Training as a counsellor can bring up lots of feelings about your own life experiences. Consider what and who will support you, most especially how you will support yourself. Identify difficulties as soon as possible and discover where and who you can ask for help for yourself. You will be learning, just as the people you choose to work with will be learning, that some problems from childhood, school and family life can travel with us. It is important for all of us to know that we can make different choices and recognise that some patterns we might have become attached to are not helping us now. You don't have to deal with difficulties on your own. It helps to share them and ask for help. These are valuable life lessons for us all.

The main purpose of this book is to throw light on the many different kinds of difficulties that can block or limit us all from reaching our potential socially, emotionally, psychologically, physically, creatively or academically.

At any age, being a student is a transition from one stage of life to another. It is a time of managing change, a time of acquiring useful knowledge and skills; these skills are transferable to the world beyond, the world of work. The word 'student' infers that you are not expected to be an expert right away! There is a mixture here of information and brief case stories to help you to reflect more on the kinds of issues that can be limiting or intimidating for us all. It is hoped that this book will help you to develop skills in yourself that support you in your choice of becoming a counsellor. It is also hoped that you will enjoy your introduction to this most inspiring and exciting work of helping and watching people grow, mature and become more comfortable with who they are.

Taking Care of Yourself

When you begin a new course of study, especially a counselling course, It is vital that you take extra good care of yourself and take time out To relax. These tips may help you to settle in to your new course.

- If you are living away from home, create an attractive working/living space with meaningful objects, pictures and books that energise you. Postcards are inexpensive; choose one that makes you smile. Take some things with you that are familiar, bring you joy, remind you of home, family and friends.

- Some students, however independent they are, can suddenly feel homesick when arriving on campus, and this can be deeply upsetting. Look out for what activities and clubs are on offer on campus that appeal to you. Stay in touch with friends and family from home. Get to know your way around where you are staying, until it becomes familiar. If these feelings continue, don't hesitate to approach the counselling service on campus yourself and talk to someone about your feelings. It may help just to book in for a half-hour assessment or you may benefit from longer-term counselling for yourself.
- Listen to music, sing, dance, enjoy sport, swimming or walking in nature, going to the theatre, visiting art galleries, whatever your interests are and whatever energises you and makes you feel good, keep these going during your time of study.
- Fresh air is important when you are sitting working on a computer, so take regular breaks outside when you can. It's good just to move around.
- Regular exercise that you enjoy, especially walking in nature. Meditation, relaxation, yoga and a healthy nutritious diet are all good ways to take care of yourself. Visit a local sports centre and see what facilities are on offer for you in your area, especially if you are staying far from home.
- Take proper breaks, whether this is a five-minute break to stretch and walk around, a day off to do something that energises you, a weekend away or a longer break. Recognise when you need a break; this is vital for your well-being.
- Quiet time with yourself. Find a comfortable and quiet place where you can sit or lie down and relax for at least 20 minutes. Find a comfortable rhythm for your breathing. Breathe in slowly and breathe out slowly. Now imagine breathing in calm, peace, whatever you need most right now, slowly and fully. Then, imagine breathing out tension, tiredness, whatever you most need to release, slowly and fully. This can relax you, especially when you are busy, and deadlines or exams are looming large!
- Sleep is important, and it is all too easy to stay up too late, too often. Catch up on sleep when you need to. It is regenerative and dreams are the best way to cleanse our subconscious and unconscious. Our nervous system is strengthened by sleep. If you are fortunate enough to be able to take short naps when you need them, that can be very energising.
- Creative pursuits can be a good way to relax. Painting, sewing, cooking, drawing, drama, listening to or playing music, photography, dancing, any form of sport, creative writing or writing a diary, even colourful doodling or colouring, any of these can be ways to express yourself and recharge your energy, even if you are a beginner.
- Playing games with friends, cards, board games, jigsaws, and computer games. Take time out for yourself to just relax and play. A counselling course can be hard work emotionally as well as psychologically.
- Massage. Any kind of massage is wonderfully relaxing. You could do a foot/hand/back massage swap with a fellow student, friend, housemate or partner.

- Soak in a hot bath, if you have access to a bath, with a candle, bubble bath, incense and music. Treat yourself. You deserve it.
- A walking meditation in a labyrinth can be very therapeutic. There are labyrinths in various parts of the country. Some are stone-built external labyrinths, and some are canvas labyrinths, used inside. You can look up a list of them on the '**Veriditas**' website to see if there is one near you. As you walk into the centre of a labyrinth, it can be therapeutic to focus on releasing anything negative, any stress, negative thoughts or feelings that may be limiting you, anything that would be helpful for you to release on your walk into the centre of the labyrinth. Once you are in the centre of the labyrinth, take some time to focus on what strength, encouragement, positive thoughts or feelings you might need to help you right now and imagine taking that into every part of you for several minutes. As you walk back out of the labyrinth, imagine bringing that positive energy with you and allow it to help you wherever and whenever you need it most.
- Contact with people, places and beliefs, organisations, activities that energise or relax you. Notice who and what gives you energy and who or what may drain your energy. This is very useful to tune into with your future clients as well.
- Laughter is a great source of energy. So, think about who and what you can have fun with.
- Buy yourself a treat, or do something nice for yourself, especially when you are busy or stressed. It doesn't have to be expensive but something fun or playful.
- Reward yourself when you achieve a particular goal.
- Think of any new activity or way of relaxing that you could do that would help you to nurture and energise yourself. Maybe something you've had at the back of your mind, 'I'd like to try that'. Just have a go.

Space to Reflect

Consider how similar fear and excitement are; sometimes they can get confused. Notice that most of us feel just the same about new experiences. Our feelings are a common link to every other human being worldwide. Feelings are a natural part of our healthy process of coping and survival, and they can be very uncomfortable. It is helpful to be able to say something positive to ourselves, '*I can do this*', '*I can cope with this*', '*I'm doing okay*', '*I'll feel better soon*'. The way we speak to ourselves is one of our best supports. We can use our creative imagination positively for ourselves rather than against ourselves. We always have a choice to see a glass or ourselves half full or half empty. We can choose to emphasise what we are doing well, our being okay, believing in ourselves, focussing on what we get right! The most important relationship we ever have is the relationship with ourselves. We can choose to be our own best friend in order to help ourselves cope well with new experiences and change. With any new course of study, we need to give ourselves as much encouragement and care as we can.

On your course, you are about to become very aware of the fact that as we grow up, we gather both helpful and unhelpful behaviour patterns. The unhelpful patterns may be outdated survival strategies; negative self-talk; old and outdated messages about ourselves or other people; limiting habits, beliefs and conditioning that can become ingrained attachments. It's part of growing up, explaining the world and knowing ourselves. Fortunately, with maturity, wisdom and self-awareness about which of these help us and which of these harm us, we can decide to change them and let some of them go. This old luggage can be heavy, too heavy. Choose what you are willing to change and just do it. Begin with one small change and then it can become easier to change any larger things. It's a bit like a room that we've been using and not clearing things away, we need to find a place for everything, and some things need throwing away! Doesn't it feel good when you have a good clear out! Come to think of it, take some time to tidy out a drawer, your bag, a file – creating order can bring you calm, peace and satisfaction.

Good Support

We all need to build good support networks, which can help us to identify a problem and sort it out. It is not helpful to talk to people who distort a situation; try to shield you from a problem or push you to deal with something you are not ready to deal with yet. You will hopefully get good support from fellow students on your course, from friends, from home, family, tutors or other friendly staff members. You may want to consider other support that may be available, from any Study Skills Centre, Library staff, Sick Bay, Medical Centre, college chaplains, teaching staff and of course any local or in-house counselling service. Take the risk to ask for help; it is there for you, and you deserve it!

Deciding to Have Counselling

It may be a condition of your counselling course, that you seek counselling for yourself. It may simply be something you decide to do as a result of feelings that come up for you on your course. Don't feel that as a student counsellor you cannot seek out counselling for yourself.

The awareness and perspective you are learning on a counselling course may cause you to want to change behaviour patterns that you begin to realise are causing you pain or discomfort. It can be about a shift in behaviour or perspective; it might be about adding more options and choices to your life; it may be that you become more aware that some aspect of your life or a particular relationship is no longer working for you anymore. It is helpful for you to think about what you might need to change, but this can be challenging as well.

Your training as a counsellor offers you the opportunity and insights to have counselling yourself in a safe and confidential space, with strong boundaries of time and professionalism to support you to be able to focus on what you really think and feel. It is powerful for you to take the time and space to hear yourself speak out, tell your story, identify what you may want to be different and then be willing to make different choices.

This experience will enable you to appreciate even more the courage and commitment of your future clients who are seeking help for themselves.

However much we know ourselves, and we are indeed the expert on ourselves, there may come a point where the perspective and experience of a fellow professional, trained to help, can be valuable to us.

We can all have blind spots, patterns, habits, attachments or behaviours that feel so familiar to us that we can't always see that they may be limiting us.

As a counsellor, I have been a witness to how far people can move forward positively in this process of counselling. Sometimes, we may need something more, perhaps longer-term counselling or psychotherapy to help identify defences that have become particularly deeply rooted. Sometimes, we may require more complex medical assistance. There are other occasions, if we are sharing accommodation with friends and fellow students, we may want to seek out help to deal with a friend or fellow student who we may be concerned about.

Within this book there is information to help you understand the many and varied reasons why people might both need and benefit from counselling. As you become an experienced professional, you can help guide your clients to be able to really listen to themselves, highlight their strengths and challenge areas where they may seem to be blocked. This will help them to move forward in a more creative and productive way.

The Assessment

Normally, when someone decides to seek counselling, they will be given an initial assessment with a counsellor who may or may not be the counsellor they will work with longer term. This initial assessment is to discuss and ascertain, where the client feels they are now and where they want to be in terms of their studies, relationships, feelings about themselves and life in general. After this assessment, the client will be assigned an ongoing counsellor, who will then see them for their regular counselling, usually hourly, for an agreed number of sessions.

Once you have completed your counsellor training and you begin to see clients, you will usually see clients who have had an initial half-hour assessment with a more experienced counsellor. Hopefully, you will receive helpful assessment notes to help you to proceed with the counselling. As you gain more experience of counselling clients, you will start to do the initial assessments with clients as well as regular counselling. These will be half-hour assessments, and you will usually be given a set form to complete. It will be very important for you to note down your first impressions of your assessment client and what they want to achieve from their counselling, which may eventually be with you or may be with another counsellor within the service you eventually work in.

Counselling is most valuable when there is a good and comfortable relationship with the counsellor, but also when both counsellor and client can be honest and challenging in the most helpful way. It is important to work in a relaxing environment that is easily accessible to the client, especially if they have any mobility difficulties or other special needs. Encourage yourself and your clients to be able to ask for help, when needed.

Encourage your clients to ask questions about anything they may be unsure about in the counselling process, especially in this initial assessment. Most important of all is that you can encourage them to feel safe and comfortable in this space and in this relationship with you. They will need to be given information, at this stage about the confidentiality guidelines which apply in any counselling relationship. It is your responsibility to make sure they can ask anything they may want to know. Your client will want to know how many sessions they are entitled to. They may want to know if their counsellor writes notes and what happens to them. They may prefer a choice of working with a 'man' or a 'woman' counsellor. They may have questions about the counselling process itself. Encourage them to ask any questions they may have about the counselling at this first assessment.

Part Two

Reasons Why People Seek Counselling

Chapter 2

Addiction – Stepping Out from the Revolving Door

Addictions Come in Many Guises

It does seem that we have an almost unlimited ability to become addicted to almost anything: shopping, gambling, over-eating, not eating, masturbation, alcohol, self-harming in many different forms, sexual violence, prescription drugs, black market drugs, work, 'helping', exercise, watching television, computer or mobile phone use, the list goes on and on. What seems to live behind addiction most of all is the compulsion to fill an emptiness, to comfort distress, to escape from 'real life' in any way we can. What keeps an addiction going are the lies and denial that we use to deceive ourselves, persuade ourselves that really all is well. Often, we can convince ourselves that we can take control if we want to. However, the truth is that it is very difficult to find our way out of addiction, and many of us will need professional help to do this.

There is another aspect to addiction that is important. This is the cynicism of the food and drinks industries that produce, sell and widely advertise products that have high levels of sugar and salt in them, which are highly addictive, to be found even in many baby foods. There was an excellent book written by Professor John Yudkin, a Professor of Nutrition at Queen Elizabeth College in London, in the 70s. The book, 'Pure White and Deadly', was informative about the harmful and addictive effects of sugar. The same is also true of salt. He refers to the fact that if you have a bowl of salted peanuts at a party next to a bowl of unsalted nuts, there is no competition; the salted peanuts all disappear, much faster! I remember being shocked when I read that St. Moritz Cigarettes, which I smoked in my teenage years, had sugar in the white filters to make them more addictive. Such cynicism?

So, although it is incumbent on each of us who experience addiction to find a way out of it, it is important to keep in mind that there are huge industries making billions of pounds out of our addictions and the laws of our land do very little to protect babies, children, young people, anyone really, from these very harmful products. One can say, we have a free choice, but do we really? These products are making a lot of money for a lot of people who know how addictive they are. The massive manipulation of the general public in terms of what we buy began to

DOI: 10.4324/9781003754244-4

escalate in the 1920s, and one of the main instigators was Edward Bernays, nephew of Sigmund Freud. He knew exactly what he was doing. This is well documented in the film *The Century of the Self.*

Edward Bernays – You Brainwashed Us!
Inspired by the film, The Century of the Self

You understood the work of your uncle, Sigmund Freud.
But, instead of following in his footsteps, working for the good
of humanity, you used his ideas in a totally different way.
You used your uncle's genius, his pioneering study of
our unconscious mind, to make yourself very rich.
You went to live in America and began to build a modern
movement of '*Propaganda*', disguised as '*Public Relations*'.

You used your uncle's discoveries of our unconscious, to develop
and industrialise a monstrous weapon of mass consumerism.
You began in the 1920s, working for a tobacco company.
Women were just not interested in buying cigarettes.
Your cynical advertising campaign pushed out images to persuade women
that smoking cigarettes would make them feel as powerful as men.
This campaign doubled the number of new women smokers.

The twisted tentacles of this propaganda, continue to reach out,
to control human hearts, minds and behaviour today.
Millions of us are brain washed with mass media advertising,
to buy and consume products known to be addictive.
Children's drinks and food laden with additives, sugar and salt.
The promotion of cigarettes, pornography, gambling and alcohol.
The compulsive use of mobile phones, social media and television.
The growth of a vast slimming industry that, far from making people
slimmer or healthier, spawns' eating disorders and low self-esteem.
Mass consumerism is destroying our health, our well-being
and it is devastating our environment, our Mother Earth.

Brainwashing

The proliferation of advertising generally brought with it a proliferation of alcoholism, addiction to smoking cigarettes and eating disorders. Soon followed by the proliferation of social media on mobile phones, which are no doubt a mixed blessing, but also bring their difficulties. Many of these things can bring about our giving attention to a world that is external to us, rather than an awareness and connection to our creative, expressive, interesting, rich, imaginative inner world.

Feeding the Wounded Child

We arrive in the world curious, playful, creative, open to giving and receiving love, joyful, healthy and happy in varying degrees. We then have a variety of needs for care and experiences that enable us to grow strong, healthy, powerful, safe, secure, curious, feeling loved, confident and feeling good about ourselves. If these needs are sufficiently satisfied, we will most likely be enabled to learn and thrive from the many and various experiences that we have.

However, things happen as we grow and develop, sometimes even at birth itself or during our childhood, that can cause us to feel wounded, traumatised, angry, deprived, hurt in some way emotionally, physically, psychologically and even at a deeper level in our higher consciousness. These deficiencies in how we are treated, or deprivations which may happen to us, can cause us to feel unsafe, insecure, weak, powerless, impotent, unconfident, unloved and many different difficult feelings.

This can cause us to build defences. Just as a tree grows in various directions, because of cuts and wounds and the light moving this way and that, we also survive by changing direction, growing towards the light or away from certain obstacles. The problem can be when we 'choose to look for something to make us feel better' and then that choice itself becomes an even bigger problem as it turns into an addiction.

It can sometimes feel as if we want to stay in 'child mode' and rely on things that look appealing, that intoxicate or comfort ourselves in the short term, but that also offers an escape from real life which is only a temporary escape from real life. A holiday that you don't want to come back from, a false high you don't want to come down from, however harmful it is. Temporarily, many dependences, addictions, habits, attachments can make us feel better but we can also continue to feel 'empty' despite the choice of 'comforter'. The core problem, trauma, emotional wounds or deprivation is not being recognised or tackled in a way that is really helpful for us. In addition, we now have a problem with the dependence, habit, addiction or attachment we have become reliant on. This 'temporary fix', will very likely prevent us from looking further inside ourselves to discover what we really need, to stop ourselves feeling 'empty' or 'unsatisfied'. This can leave us feeling increasingly 'empty', ashamed, helpless or powerless, which may in turn increase the reliance we have built on our chosen addiction, which enables us to 'numb out' from our emotions, thoughts, essentially, from ourselves. This is a very painful, vicious circle to escape from.

The first step out of addiction is to own that we have a problem, which is often the most difficult step to take with an addiction. It is hard to give up something that has become 'a crutch', 'a comforter', 'something that temporarily seems to make us feel better'. It takes courage to face the shame or fear that you may feel. It takes courage to admit that we have an addiction, and it takes maturity and a commitment to yourself to ask for help, to sign up for any kind of counselling, but it can be a very important first step out of addiction.

What can help us begin our journey to recovery is for us to even want to get better, to want to take control of ourselves again. We need to find the love inside us to want to feel healthy, strong, powerful, creative, confident and free of those compulsions that we have allowed to rule our living.

The next step is to have the courage to seek out help. You really don't have to do this all on your own. Having the courage to seek help is an excellent first step to loving yourself healthy again.

I admire this quote from Diane Mariechild in her book, *Open Mind* (Harper One), 1995.

"Every person, every creature on this planet, wants to be happy. We don't know how to make it happen.

As human beings we have the opportunity to find real happiness. Happiness comes not from denying our sadness but from opening to the sadness. We must take the risk to feel the sadness, the pain in our own lives, and the pain in the lives of all peoples. This pain will break our hearts open. When the heart is broken, the seeds of joy that have been watered by our tears will blossom".

Mending the Wounded Child

The thing is that what feels much better than a false high, constant denial or a temporary tranquiliser is being able to become really honest with yourself and by doing this, grow into your true self; the self that you were born to be; the self that you are underneath the layers of defences that you may have built around yourself; the self that you are without hiding in an addiction. Taking hold of your own will and responsibility, being your own caring, respectful, honest parent to yourself, brings rewards beyond simple escape. To grow yourself up feels amazing. To have the courage to face the truth and realities of your life is real maturity. To realise just how wonderful you are, how worthwhile you are and discover that you can survive and become stronger is humbling.

To realise that all of us have wounds from the past in varying degrees and more importantly to allow yourself to feel the pain, anger, anguish, confusion, deprivations, grief, confusion, doubt, any of the negative feelings that are simply part of being human. It is only when we are honest, real, and genuine to ourselves that we can more easily mend what has been broken in ourselves, that's a high that lasts a lifetime.

It just feels good. You don't have to do it all by yourself; get help. This is what life is about, being grown up enough to know what we might need to mend in ourselves and being strong enough to be able to ask for help. I admire enormously the clients I have worked with who have risked asking for help and who have been willing to risk exploring the trauma and hurt that they may have experienced in their lives. They have then been in a position to transform those experiences into love, strength, power, insights, maturity, joy and peace. These are the people I have found to be most evolved, compassionate, cooperative, creative, wise, humane and generous to others and exemplify the best of what it is to be human. When we acknowledge and release our emotional pain, we are put in touch with our feelings, which can act as our 'inner guidance'.

Common Reasons for Addictions: Particularly to Drugs, Alcohol or Mobile Phones

A legitimate way of searching for serenity (spirituality) and resting the mind from emotional and mental strain.

A way of reducing physical pain – accepted in some medical circles – can lead to addiction.

A way of choosing to be out of control – or expressing inner chaos.

A specific response to want to escape from chronic levels of stress, tension, worrying and pressure.

It can be that university life is developing our intellectual development to the detriment of our emotional development, and the possible distress and deprivation of this imbalance.

A transitional object – a 'substitute parent' or 'outer authority' until we find our own 'inner authority'.

Peer pressure – afraid of saying no.

Either of our parents having role modelled addiction for us.

A way of creating a ritual, which can become a substitute for something missing. particularly, drug taking may be a way of returning to some missed or desired ritual.

Creating your own community and context – a way of making friends and giving us a sense of belonging to a 'family' who have a shared purpose for coming together. This may result from the widespread and deep social 'loss of community'.

Curiosity – risk taking – how far can we take it and not get 'hooked?' This can become a power struggle between the substance versus ourself.

Freeing self from parental values – making a stand with our own generation.

Fear of responsibility of growing up and taking a full part in mature adult life – wanting to stay adolescent.

Rebellion – a 'Rebellious Child' response to perceived 'Critical Parent' experienced in childhood or a perception of the Institution as an 'authority figure' to rebel against.

A way of maintaining denial of self, denial of the seriousness of the problems, denying self-responsibility and self-care.

The chosen addiction can represent a transitional object which is not easy to let go of – especially if there is an abusive or neglectful parent who may be manifested in the drug, alcohol or mobile phone. The chosen substance may enable us to mask our problems and appear to be 'just like anyone else'. A way of repressing high energy or power – fear of realising our potential, shining our light or reaching our goals. Many of us can be afraid of how powerful and amazing we are and how much energy we could potentially have.

Addiction can become a desperate search for more energy, and some of us may try anything to renew our run-down energy. It may be, we have stopped recognising hunger, fatigue, discomfort or our need for caring and nurturing. Drug, alcohol or mobile phone addiction may be seen as a slow suicide – a desire to 'numb out from real life' destroy our presence in our own body and mind, heart. Maybe seeing our body as an adversary. Drug, alcohol or mobile phone abuse can be a downward spiral caused by a lack of motivation and concentration to do academic work. Ending up with lower grades, not going to seminars, lectures and eventually little academic work completed. It can be part of social withdrawal and isolation or only seeing our 'drug/alcohol/mobile phone group' or part of being anti-social. Any drug, mobile phone or alcohol abuse can give us a sense of being invincible but most important is that we can end up letting go of our intuition about people, which can make us much more vulnerable.

Case Story of Anton – Addiction

Anton was a French second-year computer science student. He had grown up in France, in a small town about 20 miles south of Paris. He had a younger sister of 12 and a younger brother of 15 who lived with his mother in France. His father had died when Anton was 16. Anton had wanted to study in the UK, partly to escape from family pressure for him to take over some responsibilities on the extended family farm. His mother had good family connections in the town they lived in, but he had felt an expectation from his mother and from his extended family to take the place of his father, who had been a part-time farmer and part-time accountant. Anton was not interested in getting involved in the family farm; his younger brother was the 'farmer' in the family and would be happy to take on the farm, but Anton had always enjoyed anything to do with computers. It was a huge relief for Anton to escape that unwanted responsibility.

He had an uncle who had moved to the UK some years before, and he had always got on with him. Anton and his uncle would meet up quite often. His uncle had probably influenced Anton's move to the UK as his uncle had also not wanted to go into the family business.

Anton had been thoroughly enjoying his course in his first year, but this year he was finding it difficult. He was very angry with himself because he had increasingly been drinking heavily, and his work was beginning to suffer. The truth was for him that he was terrified of becoming like his father who had been a heavy drinker.

Anton felt he was beginning to hate himself, and part of the drinking was to drown these powerful feelings of shame that he was just like his father. He felt weak and hopeless as he was now beginning to fail some of his assignments. During this year he had got involved with a group of students who nearly all drank too much and he was scared of what was happening to him. He felt powerless to stop himself.

Together we looked at his courage to come and ask for help, his awareness that there was a problem and most of all his willingness to do something about it. I asked what he felt he could and wanted to change. He decided that he needed to spend more time with the two friends he'd made the year before, whom he'd been seeing less of. Neither of them was a big drinker. He felt embarrassed and a bit immature hanging out with his 'new' friends who he really felt were not genuine friends. He felt weak because he had fallen into drinking too much.

He'd just got in touch with one of his friends from last year, and they were both keen on computers. It had been a relief to meet up with him and he had risked telling him that he had a problem and was coming for counselling. He was surprised by how supportive his friend had been.

He knew himself that he needed to see less of his 'drinking buddies', because that made him feel more like drinking, and he was beginning to hate himself. Anton was very aware, and most important for him was the feeling of not wanting to be like his father. At the same time, he felt a numbness about the loss of his father; he had found it hard to truly grieve for his father. He realised that he was angry with his father's drinking but there was a numbness in him about this too.

In his second session, we talked a lot more about his very mixed-up feelings about his father. He'd felt a mixture of numbness, anger and fear when his father died and strong feelings about wanting to 'run away', physically but also emotionally. As 'homework', he decided he needed to write a letter to his father, to express things he wished he had been able to say to him.

In the third session, he bought a letter that he had written to his father. He decided he wanted to read this out to his father, whom he placed in an 'empty chair'. Initially, he was angry with his father for 'leaving' him and the family. Anton felt he was 'trapped' into being responsible when he was too young and he was afraid of that. This anger eventually led to his expression of hidden sadness and loss that he had not really been in touch with when his father died. He was devastated by the sheer pain, not just of his father's death but the previous breakdown in their relationship because of his father's alcoholism and the huge loss of his father to alcohol. At the time of his father's death, he had felt too angry to grieve and since then he had distracted himself with coming to university and eventually his own drinking. He was surprised by the depth of grief that he felt; this was very hard for him.

In the fourth session, Anton had bought a letter, again to read out to his father, this time it contained good memories of his father and himself spending time together, when he was younger and even a walk they had done together, shortly before his death. This felt like something he needed to express in order to honour his father. He had contacted his mother to ask for a photo of his father and that felt important.

Anton felt he had probably done what his father had done, because his father had not wanted responsibility for the farm and Anton could see that there were a lot of expectations on his father from his grandparents and it had sometimes been too much for him. Hence his disappearance into drinking.

Anton had intuitively known that he needed to escape and do something different, and even coming to study in the UK had given him some distance from the pressure of family at home and his perception of their expectations. It was a pleasure to work with Anton and we arranged for him to do an occasional check-in if he felt drawn towards heavy drinking again, or just felt he needed more support. He came for a couple of sessions in the next few months but something important had shifted for him, and he was really taking care of himself and the course was going well again for him.

Chapter 3

Anger and Self-Harm – Letting It Go

Anger

There are so many different forms of anger, some that can be expressed creatively and positively. Sometimes our anger inspires us to want to change something for the better, in ourselves, or in the world around us. It can encourage us to get involved in a cause, to make something happen, which can help ourselves and others. It can also be aggressive, negative and harmful and not at all helpful to ourselves or others.

So, anger is a genuine emotion that can be used for good or ill, however expressing how we feel, and especially expressing anger can be better than suppressing it, ignoring it or pretending we aren't angry about something or with someone. If we continually suppress our anger, I believe it can harm our relationships with ourself and others. It can also be unhealthy for our physical and emotional health to deny or suppress anger. It is a good idea to think about how we choose to manage any expression of our feelings and in particularly, our anger, and be aware of what effect it can have on both ourselves and to other people.

Negative Ways of Expressing Anger

Negative ways of expressing our anger could be:

- Threatening to use weapons such as knives or guns, any physical violence is obviously aggressive and threatening
- Body language that is threatening, shaking fists, finger pointing, standing with hands on hips, raising a hand to another person, leaning in towards someone, standing too close to another person, in their space, pushing someone around and generally being a bully;
- Any form of humiliation, even using humour, designed to humiliate other people;
- Any form of discrimination against others;
- Shouting, screaming or threats of violence to intimidate someone else;
- Slamming something down onto a table or slamming doors;

DOI: 10.4324/9781003754244-5

- Using wealth, politics or power to oppress other people;
- Betrayal of confidences from other people that hurt them;
- Behaving erratically, 'hot or cold', controlling or punitive behaviour;
- Blaming other people for something that you were responsible for;
- Using a car as a weapon, for example, driving dangerously, beeping your horn aggressively, driving too close to someone, blocking the way to someone else or blinding someone with your headlights;
- Shouting, swearing or threatening to offend another person or hurt someone or their property, generally being disruptive to others in any way;
- Being a bad loser;
- Arguing, for the sake of it, being illogical and confusing;
- Ignoring other people, talking over them and pushing to be the centre of attention;
- Manipulating people and their relationships, with accusations, starting rumours, lies and deceit;
- Addictions to drugs, alcohol and food can be harmful to yourself and other people;
- Deliberately wasting resources, being destructive to or polluting our environment, just because you can, or as a way of getting attention;
- Any form of spite, oppression, abuse, persecution or punitive behaviour towards other people or animals;
- Being aggressive by pushing into a queue or a crowd;
- Refusing to accept a genuine apology from someone who may have hurt you;
- Playing psychological games, pretending or showing your anger by being silent;
- Being passive-aggressive, evasive, turning your back on someone, avoiding resolution;

Case Story of Stuart – Anger

Stuart was a postgraduate student of 25, doing a two-year part-time M.A. in Social Work. He was working on a placement with violent male offenders in the local prison, which had brought into sharp focus a fear of his own violent temper.

As an adolescent, he'd got into a few fights with other young men but he did well at school. Stuart was surprised at himself being able to get a place on a course at 'University'. He had never really had any belief in his abilities. He decided to do a degree in sociology. When he finished university, he was really unsure what he wanted to do. He went off travelling for a few years, working his way across America, which he'd enjoyed but he'd been restless and unsure about what to do next.

He came back to the UK, stayed with his mother for several months, doing various part-time jobs, to give himself time to think about what he wanted to do next. Then his father died, and Stuart inherited quite a bit of money from his father's estate. His parents had divorced when he was a teenager, and he had no siblings. He eventually decided to buy his own house with his girlfriend and come back to university to do a two-year part-time Social Work M.A. He'd got a placement working in a local men's prison.

He thought he'd maybe applied for this because his own father had been a very angry and sometimes violent man. Some part of him wanted to understand his father, but he also wanted to understand his own temper, which sometimes scared him.

He was enjoying his course, and he was now enjoying living in his house with his girlfriend, who was about to have their baby in a few months. Part of the reason for his coming for counselling was that he did not want to hurt his girlfriend or their child because of his temper. He was afraid that he could become like his father especially as he was beginning to feel stressed about having a baby and how that would change their relationship. He was afraid that the pressure from his course, from his placement, from wanting to get some improvements done in the house, could make him angry as his father had been. He was afraid of what it would be like to have a baby in the house, afraid of hurting it as his father had sometimes hurt him.

We looked at what he could do for himself to release the pressure he was feeling. He was happy to do some meditations. In fact, he realised just how tense his body was. It was incredibly difficult for him to breathe in and out deeply and relax. He realised that some of his restlessness was sheer tension. Just learning some breathing meditations made such a difference to him.

He was able to talk about the fear he'd felt about his father's temper, and he came to one session with some pictures he'd drawn of himself as a child, crouching in a corner and hiding from his father. In looking into the picture, he realised that a part of him quite often felt as if he was still hiding and crouching into a tight space.

He'd drawn a picture of a memory he had recovered of his father hitting his mother and himself hiding underneath a table. It felt as if a weight he had been carrying for a very long time had been lifted. He had begun regularly walking in the countryside around where they lived, just taking in the beauty. He had found that exercise generally was very relaxing for him.

He was able to talk about his fear of having a child and responding as his father had. He eventually talked things over with his girlfriend about how he felt and told her more about his childhood, and she had been very supportive.

We met for about five sessions over a period of two months. He had not only been able to talk to his girlfriend but also to his mother. He came for two more sessions after his baby daughter, Jessica, had been born, and he was thoroughly entranced by this little person who was his daughter.

He had become increasingly aware of any anger he began to feel and would either use a meditation to relax, play peaceful music, or sometimes just go off for a walk on his own. It had not been easy for him to tell his partner if he was feeling tense or angry but he was beginning to talk more about it and take time out to do something to release his tension. In fact, they both were becoming really good at giving each other foot massages. His partner, being really supportive of him, helped a lot.

Self-Harm

Self-harming can sometimes be hard to understand for the person doing it and for other people. It is certainly not an uncommon problem and often is a way of expressing anger. But it is often done in secret. Often people think that it is a prelude to suicide or simply a way of attracting attention. This perception can make it harder for men and women that self-harm to get the help they need. Self-harm can take many forms and can involve burning, skin picking, self-punching or punching walls or doors as well as the more common cutting or scratching.

In most situations, it is a way of releasing tension, which may have built up inside someone until it felt unbearable. It can help to limit this sometimes by releasing tension in other ways, running, punching cushions, even a cold shower can bring you back into a kind of balance. It can be dangerous if someone cuts too deep, hits too hard, but it is rarely a suicide attempt.

Because it is so often done alone and in secret, it can continue to make that person feel even more isolated and alone and can easily become a vicious circle. It can also cause the person self-harming to feel ashamed and guilty about what they are doing and make their feelings about themselves even worse. So, although it can feel like a release, it can also increase the negative and painful feeling that they may have about themselves.

I have linked this with anger for the reason that it is behaviour that can reduce a person's self-esteem hugely. It can release a variety of different difficult feelings that might feel unbearable but increase the overall hate or anger someone may feel towards themselves about hurting themselves. If it then becomes a habitual behaviour that can make them feel out of control, there is a real need for support and an increase in self-esteem to enable them to break the cycle.

The very fact of someone having the courage to seek help in counselling can help them to break the cycle and be willing to get the help they need to stop. People who do this can so often feel guilty and ashamed, and this makes it so much harder for them to tell friends or family about what they are doing. Counselling can help them to feel less alone in their difficult feelings. It is very important to accept and respect the client and help them understand the reasons for their behaviour.

Especially as this behaviour may have felt like a coping mechanism, possibly for a long time. It has been a relationship for them and will need exploring and replacing with something positive that really may support them.

Case Story of Eloise – Self-Harm

Eloise had had an assessment with a colleague, and it had been difficult for her to talk about her self-harming behaviour. She eventually shared with my colleague that she had been cutting herself, mainly on her thigh and upper arms for about a year before she came to university. When she came to university, she wanted to make a fresh start and get help to stop cutting herself. After her assessment, she'd had to wait about six weeks for her first counselling session.

After talking about it in her assessment, she'd felt strong enough to stop for a few weeks, but this past two weeks, she had begun to cut herself again. She was angry with herself and felt a bit helpless. She had spoken in the assessment about the pressure of doing A levels and getting into university as one of the triggers for her self-harming. It had helped her to talk to someone but she had missed the feeling of release, and her feelings had built up a kind of pressure inside her which she just found unbearable.

I asked her what else she had found that could give her the same feeling of release. She admitted that after her assessment she had made the effort to get out and walk around campus and go to the sports hall, played some tennis with a housemate and had joined a yoga class and both things had helped, especially the breathing exercises in the yoga. She was continuing with the class, but she had missed that 'release'. She almost felt that the cutting had become a friend, in a weird way.

I asked her to describe the image she might have of 'that friend'. She breathed out heavily and welled up in tears.

> It does feel like a way letting something out that is like a tight band of, I don't know, a restriction, a heaviness. I grew up being criticised a lot by my father, sometimes, I felt that I couldn't do anything 'right', especially for my dad.

"My brother was good at everything at school". "I was bored by what was expected, I wanted to be free".

I asked her what freedom meant to her. "I just wanted to be left alone, I loved being outside, on my swing, walking into town with my friends, just hanging out with them". "I couldn't get excited about school. I liked sport, playing tennis, running, swimming". "But that wasn't good enough for my father. I hate being cooped up and studying". Eloise was studying English,

French and Spanish, which were okay but it felt like too much. I asked her what she would like to do differently.

She really thought about it.

> I like doing English and Spanish, but I just feel that doing the French as well is too much. It feels like too much pressure and I'd like more time for doing more sport. We can have a year out, next year and I'd like to go to Spain and maybe work in a tennis school or something like that. I'd enjoy doing something more practical, and sporty.

When she talked about this, she was more relaxed in her chair, she looked excited and had more colour in her cheeks.

"It sounds to me that you have really thought about this Eloise. Could you find out more about it from your tutors and see what could be possible for your year out".

"I'd love to drop the French. I don't mind doing more Spanish classes, if I need to, I'd enjoy that so much more. I'll find out. I already feel a bit excited, just in case I can do that".

"I'm a bit afraid of talking to my father about it, he is already angry with me for not being as academic as my brother".

> He has pretty high expectations of us, which I find difficult and I guess I'm a bit rebellious too, but if I sorted it out here with the tutors and see what I might be allowed to do, that would help.

We made an appointment for a couple of weeks' time as it would take time for her to find out what was possible, and she had decided to go home in between to talk to her dad. In fact, she decided to talk to her mum first and then her dad.

I saw Eloise two weeks later and she had been busy talking to people. She had found out that because she was doing really well in her Spanish classes, she could take more Spanish classes and drop the French altogether. She'd been brave enough to tell her main Spanish tutor that she was coming for counselling. The tutor had even found some contacts about working in a Spanish tennis school as well, during her year out, which Eloise was really pleased about.

She'd had a really tough time at home with her father, but she had got her mum on side first of all. She had been honest with her father, and although he was initially angry with her for even thinking about dropping the French, he did come round. It sounded as if her mum had been helpful in all of that, eventually.

She had cut herself once at home, after she faced her father, but she then decided to tell her mum about what she had been doing, which she'd not mentioned to anyone at home before. She'd made her promise not to tell her father. She'd also told her mum that she was coming for counselling, which was a relief for her mum.

After a few more sessions which she used to talk about her relationship with her father, admitting that she had often felt controlled by him and had really buried her anger with him. Eloise was really on track for making the changes she'd wanted to do. She'd told a fellow student about her self-harming, which was very hard for her to admit to.

She was thoroughly enjoying her increased Spanish classes and was very happy to have dropped French; her course now felt manageable. She felt that the lessening of the pressure on her that she had felt, and just talking about it all, had helped her to stop cutting herself. She was very excited about having time out in Spain. We ended her counselling with the proviso that if she was tempted to cut herself again, she would come back, but it sounded to me as if she was really settling into her course, her new friends and had made some important decisions about her future.

Chapter 4

Assertiveness – I Can Do This

Being assertive means balancing a concern for others with a concern for ourselves. This is a skill that makes our communication clear and effective. It means we respect the rights of others and ourselves to say, '**no**'. We believe that we deserve to receive respect; to express views, thoughts and feelings in a manner which does no harm to anyone else or ourselves. We believe that we have the right to make mistakes. We take responsibility for our actions. We believe that we all have the right to set priorities and boundaries for ourselves; the right to consider our own needs to be as important as those of others; the right not to feel guilty when being assertive!

Someone Who Is Assertive Is Coming from a Place of I'm Okay and You're Okay

Assertive Communication

Assertive communication involves body language which matches the spoken message: an assertive person would establish good eye contact; good upright, comfortable posture, without anxious fidgeting; a strong, clear, steady voice, neither shouting nor mumbling. Being clear about specific details about time, place, context and reference. Assertive communication also involves careful and active listening, without mind-reading, assumptions and judgements. Being clear about specific details regarding time, place, context and reference. Listen carefully and actively without making assumptions and being judgemental. Check out and clarify what we understand corresponds with what was intended so that both parties share an understanding of the communication.

Assertive words include 'I' statements such as I think…, I feel…, and I want…, as well as cooperative words such as let's…, or we could…, and empathetic statements of interest such as, what do you think or how do you feel. Assertive communication is useful in most situations, unless we don't want to confront an angry person who is potentially violent. There are obviously times when it is better to walk away or be quiet!

One way to help ourselves achieve this position is to build up a positive relationship with ourselves and especially to speak to ourself in a kind and loving

DOI: 10.4324/9781003754244-6

way. It is easier to be assertive if we change some of our self-criticisms to self-encouragement and self-support. Remember that we deserve to be able to express ourselves honestly, openly and assertively. Assertive communication enables us to be listened to in the most positive way. To be an assertive person is to be able to balance one's own concerns with the rights of other people. Some of the rights we need to uphold are: the right to say NO; the right to respect; the right to express views and feelings in an appropriate manner which doesn't harm anyone else or ourselves; the right to make mistakes; the ability to take responsibility for our actions; the ability to set appropriate priorities and boundaries for ourselves; the right to consider our own needs to be as important as those of others; the right not to feel guilty when being assertive!

The alternatives are passive or aggressive communications, which surely don't work as well. However, we need all three for a moment to clearly identify the one that works best: **assertiveness**. It is vital that our body posture, eye contact and words match to get the most out of being assertive. So, try out the other two first and play with them in front of the mirror or with a friend.

Passive Communication

Passive communication can be rather self-effacing, accompanied by such mannerisms as the shifting of weight from foot to foot, downcast eyes, hand wringing, steps backwards, shrugs, a hunched body posture or a hesitant, giggly, quiet or whining voice. Passive words can include qualities such as: perhaps…, maybe…, I wonder if I could…, only…, just…, would you mind very much if…, I can't…, or fillers such as: you know…, well…, uh…, um… Also, common negative statements such as, it's not really important…, never mind…, it's all right…, don't bother.

Aggressive Communication

Aggressive communication is when someone is denying the rights of others and is typically angry, hostile or loud. It can include body language such as glaring eyes, leaning forward, pointing a finger, thumps of the fist, a sharp, sarcastic, angry, loud or dominating tone of voice. Aggressive words can include threats such as: you better…; if you don't…watch out; or discounts such as: come on; you must be kidding; and judgemental comments such as: I thought you would know better; this is your fault; don't be stupid; you're joking; **and lots of ought's, should's and must's.**

Indirect aggressive communication is when people use the language of the passive combined with body language from the aggressive communication.

Assertiveness Skills

Repetition: Calmly repeating what we want to say can help us with someone being manipulative, argumentative or distracting; we can avoid it escalating into an argument with, 'that's interesting' or we can just stick to our main point without getting side-tracked.

Responding to Criticism: Calmly admit to our critic the probability that there may be some truth in what he or she is saying, but this allows us to remain our own judge of what we do. It allows us to receive criticism comfortably without becoming defensive or explaining ourselves. This way we stay empowered.

Agreeing to Criticism: Strongly or sympathetically agree with constructive criticism of our own negative qualities enabling us to look comfortably at negative elements in our own behaviour, again without being defensive or explaining ourselves, explaining ourselves can place us in a 'child' position.

Ask for Criticism: Actively ask for criticism to use the information (if helpful) or dissipate it (if manipulative). This helps our critic to be more honest with us or assertive and less manipulative or aggressive and hence improves the whole communication. We then keep our power and empower the other person. We could offer a workable compromise to the other person if our self-worth or self-respect is not in question.

Compromise: We could offer a workable compromise to the other person if our self-worth or self-respect is not in question.

Giving Yourself Time to Think: A useful phrase if someone asks us to do something is: "I'd like to come/help, but I need to think about it and/or check my diary/ commitments". "That's interesting; I'll get back to you tomorrow/next week/later today". "I hear what you say"; Give ourself time to think.

The word, 'could': It is useful to change words like **should, must, ought** to the freedom of **could**.

Feeling okay about asking other people for help and being able to offer help to others. It is important for us to feel okay about giving and receiving compliments or thanks.

When we feel irritated by someone or something, take a deep breath and pause for a while before we react. Choose whether we want to use our energy on this or not. Save our energy for important issues.

Useful phrases if someone is attempting to escalate the conversation into a full-scale argument or wanting to leave us feeling guilty might be, "That's interesting;" "I hear what you say;" "I'd like time to think about/consider what you are saying". We do not have to explain ourselves, and to do so can sometimes be a discount of ourself. Remember other people can invite us to feel discounted or manipulated, but we have a choice as to whether we agree with them and how or even whether we respond.

The main point about assertive communication is that we and the other person both remain 'winners' and 'okay'.

How to Become More Assertive

The first stage of changing anything is to notice what we do now, so I would suggest that we take a step back from ourselves and from others and **notice** how we talk to people and how they respond. Notice how other people treat us and how they respond to us, considering the information above. Also, notice our energy around other people, who do you feel comfortable with, who gives you energy. **When we are giving or receiving aggressive or passive behaviour it can be quite a drain on our energy levels.** Self-protection is important, and there may be occasions when walking away is the best solution to avoid a situation escalating into violence or bullying.

Assertive communication and behaviour is mature, good and equal. It is a very straightforward way of communicating with other people. **It is mostly energising because there is an equal exchange of energy,** which leaves neither person drained. This style of behaviour and communication is most likely to leave us feeling positive about ourselves and about the other person.

After a time of 'noticing' we can make a choice to change something about our communication or behaviour, one step at a time. We could choose to focus on being particularly assertive for one hour of the day, or with a particular person, or over a particular event or occasion. Change is better tackled in small 'bite size pieces' at first. Allow ourselves to notice and feel good about any changes we make.

If you have a particular situation in mind where you want to be assertive it can help to do a role-play. Set up two chairs and role-play, in turn, being yourself and the other person. Notice what it feels like to give and receive assertive communication. You could ask a friend to help you. Role-plays are empowering and are an excellent way of being prepared.

Case Study of Michelle – Assertiveness

Michelle is an international student from Italy studying law as her major subject and languages as her two minor subjects. She has enjoyed her first year, especially the part of the course which involves studying languages, but she is finding the beginning of the second year a real trial. She is unhappy and is beginning to fail some of her law assignments. She really wants to either leave university or change from doing law to just languages, which she is really enjoying. She is afraid to tell her parents. Their expectations have always been that she would join her father's law firm in her home country when she qualified.

In the counselling, she describes her second year as trying to wade through a muddy swamp, even though she's always been a high achiever.

She enjoyed the first year, studying in a different country, different culture, different language, but she is finding that she is less and less interested in studying law. It doesn't inspire her, and the idea of joining her father's law firm at home has become less and less appealing. She had thought that once she was here and studying, it would all come right for her and she would find an area that interested her, but she hasn't. She's afraid to talk to her parents about it, and now she's beginning to fail some of her law assignments, which will be even harder to explain away to them.

In the counselling, she acknowledges that a part of her is angry about their expectations, and the hard bit for her is that she just doesn't know what else she wants to do. We talk about what ideas she has had previously at school or when talking to friends, but it is so hard for her to think of what she wants to do rather than what she doesn't want to do. She seems quite passive-aggressive and does a lot of 'yes, but'. Whatever other people have suggested, she always has a reason for not wanting to do it.

She likes new experiences, travel in particular. She has been much more excited about travelling to and living in the UK than the course itself. She likes people and is good at different languages. She acknowledges, really for the first time, that law is not her thing. It has been a family expectation, and she has been scared to tell her parents that she really is not very interested in working as a lawyer. The more she studies it the less it is of interest. So, the challenge for her is how to assert herself with her parents.

We discuss her doing more research about what does appeal to her, and she decides to go to the Careers Office to get more information from someone who might link the things she enjoys and is good at. She's willing to talk to her parents but wants to have an alternative in mind. This seems a very good idea.

She gradually builds up a picture of what she wants to do. She has decided to increase her commitment to her language courses, which she is thoroughly enjoying. She has been enjoying studying English and French for some years, and now she enjoys that ancillary part of her degree course and is doing very well in these. She has found the Careers Office very helpful and now feels it is the right time to approach her parents.

In some situations, she is assertive and able to stick up for herself, but facing her father is difficult. So, we look together at what she wants to say.

We do a few role-plays of how she could assert herself and be honest with him. Yes, he may be angry about her giving up studying law or leaving the course, but would he really want her to continue doing something she just isn't connecting with or enjoying?

She's grown up conforming and pleasing other people, and part of her is devastated at the idea of letting down her father. She had initially felt very scared, but in talking it through, she realised that, hidden even from herself, she feels angry about a future that has been mapped out for her, and at some level, she even feels relieved to have failed some of the law assignments. She feels now she could begin by being honest with everyone. She decides to talk to her mother first about what has happened and why.

She knows it will be difficult, but she also believes that her father loves her enough to accept her decision to change course and career if that is what she really wants. She decides to make a trip home to sort this out and although she is anxious, she has found the strength to be more honest with her parents. It was hard for her to come and ask for help. There is a new confidence about her, a determination. She is much more vocal about what she doesn't want to do, and she has a real motivation to come back and study languages and see where that takes her. That seemed like a good place for her to begin!

Chapter 5

Bereavement – The Path of Your Tears

Coming to Terms with Loss

You may work with a client who is experiencing a family member or friend who is terminally ill, and you may be helping them to come to terms with their feelings about this potential loss. They may need help from you to decide if they take time out from their course to spend at home and help to decide how they can best tell tutors and get help to ask for compassionate leave from their department at this time.

The death of someone close to us can be one of the most painful events of our lives. This is especially difficult for anyone at university who is living away from home, family and friends, who would normally support them and share this experience. Also, it may be their first experience of bereavement, which can be particularly hard to cope with.

There is such pain in grief and loss but it is a pain that joins all human beings together, since universally, most of us experience at some time, the loss and grief of losing people we care about. It may, of course, be a different kind of loss, loss of country, job, health, limbs, anything that we love, value or need. It is part of our essential humanity to experience many different kinds of losses. We need to encourage our clients to give time and respect to the process of grief and hopefully a gradual acceptance of the pain of it.

There are normal feelings one experiences when someone close to us dies, firstly grief, but also maybe anger, sometimes with yourself, especially if you are far away, sometimes an anger with the person who dies. Sometimes there are powerful feelings of being abandoned by the person who has died, even anger with other people involved, doctors, other medical staff, anyone else who may have seemed to have caused the death in some way, even anger with a 'higher power' for allowing this to happen at all.

It takes time for us all to begin to accept the powerful feelings of experiencing the death of someone who is important to us. It is crucial to encourage our clients to be understanding and gentle with themselves.

It can be hard for our clients, especially on a university campus, or still at school, as many people around them may never have experienced the death of someone close to them. Friends may mean well but may not know how to respond to such a

DOI: 10.4324/9781003754244-7

loss. People can often say things that aren't helpful: 'Cheer up', 'You should have got over it by now', 'At least you still have...'. There may be other friends who try to 'cheer them up', by dragging them along to a night out, which might be what they want, but really may not be helpful at all.

A bereavement can make it hard for our clients to concentrate on work for a while, so do encourage anyone in that situation to let their tutors and lecturers know if they need more time allowed for them to do assignments. Many such clients may also need to take extra time out to go home to stay with their family.

As counsellors, we become very experienced at working with students and staff who have experienced a bereavement and understand how important it is to take the time and the space needed to reflect and talk about these difficult feelings. There may also be practical matters that need to be dealt with. It can really help to have counselling to talk all of this through.

Some counselling services offer bereavement groups so that students, who might find it helpful, can meet fellow students who have had similar experiences. Such groups can really help and support each other to take the time needed to come to terms with such a deep loss.

Actions, Some Clients, Experiencing a Bereavement, Have Found Useful

It may be helpful for some clients to create a shrine in their room, to dedicate to someone they have lost. To create a space where they can put a photograph or something memorable about the person they have lost, place flowers, light a candle and regularly give time to meditate or just think of what that person has been to them.

If there is something left unsaid for them, with the person who has died, it can help some clients to write a letter to the person who has died. In the writing of it, they are expressing something that may be important for them to say. The client could role-play reading out this letter to them in an empty chair in the counselling room. It may help your client to imagine their words being heard.

It may be that your client needs to value gifts they have received from the person who has died. You could suggest that they wrap some empty boxes, large or small, in colourful paper and that they can even write on each box, a gift that they felt they'd received from them. Keeping these in a special place, for as long as they may need, can be an important part of expressing their respect, gratitude, love or remembrance.

If your client lives close to a church, cathedral, a labyrinth or any special place of remembrance, they can be places for contemplation and for a walking meditation. A place where they can remember and honour the person who has died and acknowledge the importance they have been in their lives. They could do this on their own, or take someone with them, who will support them.

There can be many different losses in our lives, and it is important and valuable for clients to get help to talk through how they are feeling. For some of our clients, it might be leaving school and home or even country and beginning at university, it is after all a big change. Some students may have parents who separate or divorce, while they are at university and this can be very difficult to accept. Failing exams can be a real loss and a disappointment. If a family member, or even a favourite pet, dies at home while they are away at university, it can be hard for them not to be able to share this with their family.

It may be that, while a student is away at university, their family moves to a different house, location or even country. For some students, this can be difficult and may take time to accept. Becoming ill, injured or disabled in some way can be a shock and a loss, especially if you are far from home. Counselling can be an important support to get anyone through a significant change or loss in their lives.

Coming to Terms with a Terminal Illness

Sadly, there are occasions where a student is faced with a diagnosis of a terminal illness during their studies at University. This is obviously a very stressful and difficult situation for anyone to face. Counselling can help someone in this situation to come to terms with their diagnosis, to express their feelings, especially to be able to express any fears they have about dying. It is important to enable anyone in this situation to think about what their needs are emotionally as well as physically and practically at this time. There may be decisions that they have to make about their treatment. If they haven't yet told their family and friends. They may want to discuss how they tell their family, friends or other people about what is happening to them.

They may have to decide how long they can stay on campus. If they need to leave university, it may be helpful for them to consider where they want to go and what type of care and support, they will need and want to receive.

It may be too early for them to think about practical details, but some people can feel reassured by being informed about local available palliative care or organisations that can help, such as: Death with Dignity; Macmillan Cancer Support; Mariecurie.org.uk; and others.

They may want to consider questions about: Would, they want to die at home? In a hospice? It may be too soon to talk over practical details, but they may want to talk about practical things like: What kind of funeral do they want? Have they made a will? Do they want a burial, cremation, green funeral, other alternatives? What is most important to them at this time?

Case Story of Arjun – Bereavement

Arjun had been referred by his tutor, always a good student; he had just stopped handing in work and going to seminars, lectures. His tutor called him in to see him and persuaded him to come along for counselling. Arjun sat quietly, little energy in his face or body. He shrugged his shoulders when

I asked why he had come. He looked out of the window and avoided any eye contact. After a while, he almost whispered, "I just thought she'd always be here". "I need to be with my family, but I have mid-term exams". "I can't concentrate, I feel empty inside, I just can't be here".

Arjun then talked about his grandmother, who had been ill for some months and was now dying. She was a main caring figure in his life, with both his parents working full time as doctors. He shared memories of her. He thought deeply about his needs. Then, we sat in silence together for some time. He decided that he must be with his parents and the rest of his family. This was important. As soon as his decision was made, he looked stronger, determined. Arjun decided to notify all his lecturers and ask for their help to extend deadlines and get updates on the lectures he would miss.

It helped him to ask for support from his lecturers, and they were very understanding. They enabled him to be able to take some time out to go home to his family, which was very important for him.

He decided to come back and have some sessions of counselling after her death. In this ongoing counselling, he acknowledged what a great loss this was for him and how important it had been for him to go home and spend time with his, 'Nani', and be with his family during this time. It helped him to share his feelings of sadness and grief. He talked about what he needed to do now, to honour her.

Luckily, we had a labyrinth on campus, ideal for meditation. Arjun found it helpful to walk in the labyrinth a few times. He imagined himself walking with her by his side. At the centre of the labyrinth, he imagined that he was able to take into his heart, what she had been for him, her strengths and her presence and let go of what he'd found difficult about her. It was important for him to take time to grieve for her. He came along for seven sessions of counselling, sometimes, he needed to sit in silence and sometimes he just wanted to remember things about her, especially her constant presence in his childhood and her kindness to him. He expressed his anger at her not being there anymore. He was surprised by that. He shared many of his memories and honoured her in silence. He found peace in this.

Most important for him, as she had been unconscious when he had visited her before her death, he decided to write her a letter expressing what he would have liked her to know, if she had been conscious. He decided he wanted to read this out to an empty chair where he imagined her to be. This was very powerful for him, and he felt it had really made up for the loss of being able to say a proper goodbye to her. He decided to create a small shrine to her in his room, with a beautiful photograph of her, which he shared in the counselling. He lit a candle for her twice a day for a couple of months and felt he was truly able to honour her in his own special way.

Case Story of Darren – Loss

Darren was a first-year student studying accounting. All Darren had ever wanted to do growing up- was play football. He was talented and had been assured of a career ahead of him as a footballer, until he broke his leg in a skiing accident, a year ago, on a school trip. This injury had ongoing difficulties that meant he couldn't play football anymore. Darren's parents had persuaded him to think about going to university to study accounting, which he was good at, and he had eventually decided to do that.

He came for counselling because, although he was beginning to enjoy university life, it bought up feelings about the potential career he had lost. For months, he'd just felt sick about not being able to play football. He had been the best player all the way through school and 18 months ago, he had eventually been accepted into one of the top football clubs' early training school, run by his dream team. He had been bitterly disappointed, it was such a big loss for him, he was very down about it, but also very angry, and was still, understandably, finding it difficult to let go of 'what could have been'. Coming to university had somehow made it worse, the realisation that his dream was never going to happen.

He'd begun drinking too much, something he'd never done before, and he was worried; it was getting worse. He sat in silence for a bit and said he just felt numb. As the silence increased, he shuffled his feet and began to cry. He just kept saying over and over, "it's so unfair". He described his feeling of emptiness. He just couldn't grasp the loss of his dream, it had been just in reach for him, and now it was gone, forever. He described, not knowing how he could really cope with this huge weight of disappointment. He almost wished he had never had such an amazing opportunity in the beginning. It just made it worse to know what he'd lost. Although he'd felt sad, since he realised he would never be able to play football professionally, the reality of coming to university and having to choose a different path for himself, had increased his feelings of loss.

Darren sobbed and said, "I just don't know how to let go, it feels, just too big". "I know drinking isn't an answer, it doesn't really help. I'm so angry with myself for going skiing and doing this to myself. I just can't accept how stupid that was, how stupid I was". I asked him if he could forgive himself for having an 'accident'. It wasn't a choice he'd made; it was a genuine 'accident'. Darren cried again, angry tears. He cried out, "I can't blame anyone but myself". I asked him if he would blame someone else, a friend, a family member, for 'having an accident'. He thought about it and said, "No, I probably wouldn't". We sat in silence for some time. He shook his head. "I guess, I must just learn to forgive myself". He almost smiled.

I asked him what might help him to express the huge disappointment and loss. He thought about it and said, "the only way he might be able to express it was to paint his feelings". He explained that he'd always enjoyed drawing and painting as a child, and sometimes when he'd been frustrated in the past, it had helped him to paint how he felt. He hadn't painted anything for a long time.

I suggested, as 'homework', that he might like to paint a picture of how it had felt for him to be chosen to be in the training team, how it felt now, and how he might envision a future without playing football.

In the next counselling session, he brought two medium-sized paintings wrapped in brown paper and was a little shy about showing them to me. He'd decided to have a go at expressing what he felt inside.

The first one he unwrapped was very good. It was one of him playing football at the club in the young training team, it showed his joy. He was jumping in the air and kicking the ball high into the corner of the goal. He looked so powerful. As he showed me this painting, he was proud, and it was obvious that he was a good artist and had been a talented footballer, with realistic expectations of a career in football. He rested the first painting up against the table and unwrapped the second painting, which was slightly bigger.

He unwrapped it, with a tense, sad and very pale face. This painting depicted the main team playing on the pitch, and he was sitting in the audience watching, his leg in a large white plaster cast. In the centre of the painting was a huge, violent black strike of lightning cutting through the painting. This second painting was powerful. He looked at it through tears, and he was shaking. The painting was both angry and sad. In the painting he looked as he looked now, tense, sad and pale. He rested this painting against the table next to the first one. He cried as he looked at both the paintings. It was as if he was saying goodbye to his absolute dream. From a small boy, this was all he had thought about. He was devastated at having to give this up, especially as he had really been on track to succeed. He told me that before he decided to come for some counselling, he had thought seriously about harming himself. It just seemed as if there was nothing left to live for. There was just a black hole for him.

He was very upset, but it felt as if in this painting, he was very well able to express the anger and the huge loss he felt. We sat in silence for some time, and the room felt full of grief. The black lightning strike perfectly expressed his devastation. We both sat, honouring that young man in the painting and his dream.

He told me that he couldn't yet paint the third picture, the future felt blank. He realised that it would take time to let go of all this, and he appreciated having somewhere to come where he could really express his feelings. He just couldn't yet see what it might be like at the other side of these painful feelings. He was a very aware young man, and I really felt for his pain.

Before he left, he told me he had been getting good marks in his latest accounting project; it had begun to lift him. It was the first positive thing he had talked about since the counselling began. I asked him to think about, what might be a good outcome for him after leaving university. He thought about it, almost not daring to say anything. Then, he told me that he had thought of trying to get a job, at 'the club', doing some sort of job in finance there, but this time, I'm not going to set my heart on anything and see how it goes.

In Darren's last counselling session, he came in with another small painting wrapped in brown paper. He was grinning and looked 'lighter' in some way. He gave it to me to unwrap. I unwrapped it, and it was a small painting of him working in an office that had on the wall 'Arsenal Football Club'. He had decided to talk to his old trainer and see if they would consider him to work in the office at the club when he finished his degree, if he got a good result. He told me, "I'm not putting pressure on myself, but there is no harm in asking", and he was determined to do well now, whatever happened next. Darren was basically a positive person, and I felt sure he would make other dreams come true for himself, whatever they might be.

Chapter 6

Cultural Diversity – Valuing Difference

Identity

It is important that we focus on our need to have a sense of belonging and what cultures we identify with, in terms of not only race but also gender, religion, age, education, class, etc. Many of us will have experienced the role of both oppressor and oppressed at some time in our lives, and identifying such experiences allows us to have more understanding of the subject as a whole. It is important to take more risks in confronting the fear we often feel within, when confronting, in an honest way, racial or cultural differences. This is vital when we are seeing so many students from different cultures and backgrounds. It is important to encourage training in this area. So many misunderstandings and feeling of mistrust and isolation are based on a lack of cross-cultural awareness.

When we consider aspects of culture and our inner being, it can be so much easier to share the similarities and how difficult it can be to acknowledge differences, where racial, sexual, class, religious and other differences occur. It is important to consider our attitudes and beliefs, past and present, and how difficult it may be to change such beliefs and how this affects our work with clients. It is immensely human to seek a sense of belonging and how this can affect our attitudes to perceived differences in other people. Culture can be seen to be like skin – a tension between external and internal conscious and unconscious influences. We are so often afraid of risking, of being wrong, and this can lead to our seeking out similarities rather than differences in other people.

Differences

It is important to consider how many students sit in seminars with skills to offer, points of view not expressed, intellectual ability not realised, often due to lack of confidence, lack of perceived power. This is not only a loss to them, as individuals, but it is a loss to the group and to the Institution. I have often heard non-white students admit to feelings of isolation, caused by wariness and distrust displayed to them by non-black students. We have a responsibility to encourage as many students as possible to express their personal power, and that is enabled by valuing our

DOI: 10.4324/9781003754244-8

diversity and differences. I have often heard both non-white students and women students express feelings of not feeling included in seminar discussions.

The Challenges and the Changes

Two quotes from an excerpt of a Working Paper 189 entitled, 'White Privilege and Male Privilege: A Personal Account of Coming to See Correspondences through Work in Women's Studies' (1983), written by Peggy McIntosh, an associate director of the Wellesley College Centre for Research on Women. This small section was entitled 'White Privilege: Unpacking the Invisible Knapsack':

> One factor seems clear about all of the interlocking oppressions. They take both active forms, which we can see, and embedded forms, which as a member of the dominant group one is taught not to see. In my class and place, I did not see myself as a racist because I was taught to recognize racism only in individual acts of meanness by members of my group, never in invisible systems conferring unsought racial dominance on my group from birth.
>
> To redesign social systems, we need first to acknowledge their colossal unseen dimensions. The silences and denials surrounding privilege are the key political tool here. They keep the thinking about equality or equity incomplete, protecting unearned advantage and conferred dominance by making these subjects taboo. Most talk by whites about equal opportunity seems to me now to be about equal opportunity to try to get into positions of dominance while denying that *systems* of dominance exist.

I have to include a quote from Nelson Mandela, who had every reason to hate, serving so many years in prison but instead he learnt about love.

> No-one is born hating another person because of the color of his skin, or his background, or his religion. People must learn to hate, and if they can learn to hate, they can be taught to love, for love comes more naturally to the human heart than its opposite. 5 Jun 2020.

Fortunately, universities are full of students from so many different countries and diverse cultures that they are ideally institutions that have the potential to educate students about cultural diversity and the real power of valuing difference.

Case Story of Rose – Valuing Difference

Rose had been for a half-hour assessment with another counsellor, and she was now coming for her first full counselling session. In the assessment, she had talked about feeling depressed and not really coping well with her workload. This was her first time studying abroad. She was from Johannesburg, and it was her first long stay away from her family, whom she really missed. There were quite high expectations of her from her family as she was the first family member to go to university. In the assessment, she had talked to the counsellor about feeling not only depressed but quite afraid of not being able to cope here.

Rose took up so little space in her chair. She was a young and attractive black woman, smartly dressed, with glasses. I asked her how she was doing. She began to cry a little, took her glasses off and wiped her tears. She smiled and apologised, and I told her there was no need to apologise. She sounded quite down and told me the work was going okay, her housemates were okay, but she just really missed home, her family. She had liked the idea of studying abroad and particularly in the UK but the reality was that she felt a very long way from home.

At first, she'd been really excited, her first trip to Europe and the UK. But everything was so different. She was doing computer studies for her course and that was okay, but it all felt so unfamiliar. She was homesick but it wasn't really that. I suggested she take her time, and she relaxed in her chair a little.

"I guess I'm a bit scared of being in the UK, everything smells different, looks different, feels different. All the other students seem to know what to do". I asked her what she was scared of. She didn't really think she was good enough. She looked down at her lap and said softly, "Most people are 'very white' here". I asked how that made her feel. She began to cry. "I didn't know I would feel like this". "I just really miss my family, my home, even my country. It is all so different here". I asked if she knew any other new students who were from South Africa. "I've met one young black South African man who is from Cape Town, and someone told me there were two black South African women from Johannesburg a few houses away, but I haven't seen them and I have been too shy to look them up". I asked if she would make the effort to contact them, as it may help. She agreed.

I reminded her that there will be many different international students from all over the world who are going to be feeling just like her. She grinned, "I have high expectations of myself, that I can do anything, which sometimes scares me". "That sounds like you like an adventure". "You're right, I do".

I asked if she was enjoying the classes. She began to cry again. "I'm a bit scared of thinking I can do this here in the UK". I asked what she meant. "Well, I didn't know I'd feel like this, but in South Africa, I suppose I do still feel a bit second class to white people". "I didn't know I would feel like that, because it is different now in South Africa, but I do. I find myself looking away from people, feeling not good enough to be here". "In South Africa, when I was growing up there were layers of different people who were seen as better than, lower than". "I didn't know I would feel like that, but weirdly, I do. I remember that kind of thing from when I was little and coming here, makes me remember".

"What would help you with that?" "Well, just saying it to you, makes it sound a bit crazy". "It's not crazy if that is how it was for you then, there's a memory of that inside you". "Maybe, you can give yourself a bit of a break and realise it may take time for anyone coming to another country to get used to it, but what you experienced as a child was something else".

> "Yes, it was and I suppose it has left its mark on me, maybe that's one of the reasons I needed to come and study here. Somehow to lay to rest that feeling that I am 'lesser than'. It takes a long time to go away when it is so ingrained in a whole 'system'. I don't think I've realised how much it has affected me".

"I hope being here can help you Rose. That system of apartheid was abusive".

"Yes, it was, I have many memories that I think I want to wipe clean"

"Then I hope that your time here can help you to do that".

We made an arrangement to meet up the following week. I asked her to be a little kinder to herself this coming week and maybe talk to other people more about how they are getting on. We both agreed that it was a pretty big thing just to settle into university, let alone be so far from family and home.

Rose came for two more sessions, and she gradually settled in, made friends with the two South African young women who had grown up in Johannesburg. She had housemates who were from the UK, France and Sweden. They were all getting to know each other. Her housemates, particularly wanted to know about South Africa and openly asked about apartheid, which surprised her.

In the counselling, she wanted to address having been given a feeling of being 'lesser than' around white people in South Africa, and so it was a bit weird coming to the UK. She was able to talk about it, remember situations that just didn't make sense to her. It gave her a sense of inferiority, which she wanted to let go of. I asked her what would help her to do that? "I think that's why I wanted to come here, to the root of those feelings". I asked her, if that had helped her. "I think it gradually is changing something for me, coming here. I just feel like a normal student, learning to fit in. I didn't expect that".

I asked how she felt about me being a white counsellor. She was very able to get in touch with her feelings. "She felt initially, when she came into the room, maybe she wouldn't trust me, I would see her as 'lesser than". She asked me straight. "Do you see me as less human, less valuable than you". I replied, "I really don't. I see you as different than me because you have grown up in a different country, but as a human being I see you as 'like me', as a woman, I see you as 'like me'. Does that answer your question". Rose laughed, "I have always wanted to ask a 'white person' that". She really laughed, we both laughed. She was a delight.

In her last session, she was much more relaxed. She talked more about her course, what she was doing. She really enjoyed studying computer science. She had made quite a few friends. Her housemates were great. They all shared a love of films and music. I asked her, if she intended to go back home, what work did she want to do. She really enjoys studying computer studies, and she has already decided to set up her own company in Johannesburg. I wasn't at all surprised. It felt like her curiosity brought her to the UK, and that seems to lead her through her life. Rose is a powerful woman who just wants to learn more and more about life.

Chapter 7

Depression – Moving Out of the Tunnel

Depression

Feeling depressed is very frightening, especially if you don't know why. I am not talking here about clinical depression, which can be extremely debilitating, but a deep sadness. Many clients who come along and say they are depressed or 'down' have very good reasons to feel that way, maybe because they feel something is missing in their lives now or was missing in their early lives. Depression is often related to loss, repression or suppression. It can be about the absence of 'good enough parenting', 'good enough loving', 'sufficient caring, support, recognition, security or safety'. It is the sense of something important missing that children ideally need in their early lives. Depression can involve a sense of being deprived. Many people are unaware of or uncomfortable talking about such feelings. Counselling is about increasing our awareness of and connection to our inner self and particularly being more aware of our many and various feelings.

Feelings can lie dormant inside us, waiting for a time when we feel strong enough to express them. When we are going through a time of great emotion, it can be a defence or coping mechanism to repress the strength of our feelings at that time. It is very freeing to allow awareness of 'old emotional luggage' and give ourselves a chance to gain emotional maturity, strength and insight.

Such feelings can often feel as if they are hidden deep in a tunnel of feelings, which may be fear, sorrow, guilt or anger in varying degrees. We can easily find ourselves going round in a revolving door at the entrance to the tunnel because to go deeper into the feelings is scary, and we are not sure where it may take us. Many of us don't trust our feelings, and it is true that feelings are uncomfortable, inconvenient and not always easy to contain. There is often the fear that we could tip into becoming out of control. However, I have often sat with people who have allowed themselves to feel a place inside them that may feel desperate, sometimes a hugely deep pool of sadness, but they always manage to come back to a calm and centred place afterwards. Often it is a tremendous relief to visit that place and know you are okay in doing so.

Our feelings are the only thing that I believe is totally common to all people and cultures of the world. Most human beings know varying strengths of sadness, fear,

DOI: 10.4324/9781003754244-9

anger and often joy and happiness. It is something that is our human birthright to have our feelings. In this way, we are truly connected to every other human being. There is indeed a dignity in knowing and expressing our true feelings. It is a positive step nearer for us to knowing ourselves and each other better.

Low-Level Depression

I would also describe this as a kind of joylessness. What is it that young people are searching for when they steal a car and drive it around at speed? They are certainly chasing the buzz, the excitement, even notoriety with their friends, 'street-kred', even, in the case of some young men, a recognition of their masculinity. I also think they are chasing something to take them out of joylessness, something to help them to feel good and feel alive.

Childhood has increasingly become about performance, being judged and criticised as a preparation to become a future commodity in the world. There is often little time for nurturing that sense of wonder in the world and even less time and space for nourishing the joy and happiness in our lives. Some young people are being daily stressed and pressurised by the expectations on them.

Many of the young people I have seen for counselling in a university setting are so focussed on performance goals, often high expectations from their family and from themselves. This can create fear of the future and can squeeze the joy out of their lives. There can be a frantic quality in their time out with friends, sometimes involving excess drugs or alcohol to capture the impression of joy.

Then there is the passive way of spending a lot of time on social media or television watching other people doing things. This can increase a way of numbing out from 'real life' and the joy of being active, creative and involved in initiating joyful activities for yourself.

It is important for us all to question whether how we spend our time and energy really brings us joy, increases our energy, our power, our confidence and sense of well-being.

Case Story of Jonathan – Depression

Jonathan was a young man, dressed in a lot of black, who was becoming increasingly isolated at university. He hardly made eye contact with me, often looking at the floor. His eyes were inward and lonely, his head, arms and legs all seemed to gravitate towards the floor. He had been sent by his doctor, who had prescribed antidepressants, but also felt Jonathan needed counselling. He had made one or two friends last year, one of whom had recently left University and he had a good childhood friend living in his hometown, who came to stay very occasionally but he was going out less and less often and was losing his motivation to do his academic work.

At some point, I usually ask clients to tell me about themselves from as far back as they remember, including what they might have been told about their birth experiences. I believe we pick up messages and feelings not only from babyhood and how we experience our entry into the world but sometimes even during our time in the womb. Certainly, Jonathan knew that his mother had suffered post-natal depression after his birth and again after his younger sister was born, when he would have been three. His mother recovered fully from this post-natal depression, and there was no other family history of depression. However, depression would have been an emotional response that Jonathan would have been familiar with from an early age.

Jonathan remembers that he occasionally would have periods of feeling down as a child, but he really started to feel a deeper depression at about 16 when he felt coerced by his teachers and parents into the direction of taking subjects at school leading to a science degree. He was good at these subjects but was not particularly interested in the idea of doing science. He felt a bit as though his career was being mapped out for him. Jonathan felt he had just given in. In doing so, he had lost respect for himself in allowing himself to be forced down a path that other people wanted for him.

It took a few weeks to discover that Jonathan harboured a real passion for dancing and would have liked nothing better than to become a professional dancer. I was astounded by the animated expression and energy on his face when he talked about dancing. Jonathan was initially reluctant to talk about it, thinking that I would be like the rest, seeing it as a 'no hope' profession. His parents had put enormous pressure on him to give up dancing during his GCSE examinations so that he could concentrate on his schoolwork. He had never really talked through this loss of something, which he had loved passionately from a child. He had started lessons by accident when his sister went to ballet, and they had needed more boys in the tap-dancing class held at the same time. He took to it like a 'duck to water'. Part of his 'homework' from the counselling was to find out if there was a dance school near campus that he could join and at least enjoy it in his spare time even if he didn't intend to continue with it as a career.

Jonathan had experienced giving up his dancing as a huge loss in his life. He couldn't face seeing any of his friends from the dance school at home as he felt humiliated at allowing his parents to dictate to him about his life in such a way. He missed the excitement and enormous sense of achievement he had experienced when he won competitions and helped to arrange shows. He admitted that he often jotted down choreography for certain pieces of music when he became bored with his academic work. It was only when Jonathan began to feel his stored-up sadness and anger that he realised how important his passion for dancing was still. The light at the end of Jonathan's particular tunnel of feelings was a determination to get back something he loved.

The following week he had discovered that there were no suitable classes on campus, but he found an excellent dance school a train ride away, and he visited them right away. They were so impressed with his experience and abilities that they asked him to do some teaching of a young class as well as joining in on some adult dance performances. One of the teachers there was in the process of setting up an innovative new dance group and, when she heard about his previous experience, she asked him if he might be interested in helping with the choreography for the group as well as joining in the dancing. It sounded as if he was very experienced and had found a place where his talents might be recognised.

He decided to continue with his science degree so that he would always have that to fall back on in case things didn't work out in the world of dance. The difference was that he decided to have both things in his life and the dancing might help him to find more interest in the science, at which he was pretty good. Jonathan looked so much freer and more alive in his face and body once he had reclaimed this very important creative source of expression in his life. Instead of a tunnel, Jonathan described the counselling as having been like a car wash. He described the tears he had shed, and there had been many, as having washed him clean and having enabled him to start again on his journey out into the world!

When we bury our feelings or passions, it can feel like we are making a part of ourselves disappear. Sometimes, it is only by recognising and knowing how strong our feelings are that we can truly know who we are and what we want in the world.

Chapter 8

Disability or Long-Term Ill Health – You've Got Here

Asking for Help

We would often see students in the counselling service with some debilitating chronic illnesses, such as ME (Myalgic Encephalomyelitis), also known as Chronic Fatigue Syndrome (CFS) or Fibromyalgia (FMS). These illnesses often affect a variety of body systems. One of the prime symptoms can be long periods of extreme fatigue that don't always improve with rest or sleep but are often made worse by mental and physical activity. This fatigue can be accompanied by physical unsteadiness, pain and by a sense of 'brain fog'.

Occasionally a younger student, but more often a mature student may develop the early onset of Parkinson's disease. This is a progressive nervous system disorder causing decline in brain function, which can gradually worsen and cause a variety of symptoms which can impede movement, particularly balance and speech and is usually increasingly debilitating. This can be a hugely distressing diagnosis as, at present, there is no apparent cure. In recent years, there have also been students with a diagnosis of 'Long Covid' and of course, there are a variety of other distressing health conditions that may cause students to seek the support of counselling.

Although these clients would be getting medical help and other practical and physical supports, some students would be referred to the counselling service when the emotional effects of such long-term illness can simply be overwhelming, depressing and frustrating. These illnesses can often affect multiple body systems. Facing up to such debilitating illnesses can be extremely hard, especially for a young person, surrounded by other young people who are often at their peak of good health. Counselling can really help students deal with the shock and the ongoing distress of such a long-term, serious diagnosis. There can be enormous pressure when combining university work with just coping with the day-to-day energy lapses and feelings of being unwell. This can be overwhelming for them. Also, such long-term illnesses can obviously be very difficult for friends, family and long-term partners.

Occasionally, it can be the sheer frustration of not being able to find a way out to wellness and good health and having to accept that their condition is getting worse,

DOI: 10.4324/9781003754244-10

or just not really getting better, over a long time period. The frustration and disappointment of this can sometimes be helped by talking it over with a counsellor, beginning to accept the basic premise, that there may, at least, be good days and bad days. We have an expectation in society that if we become unwell there is most often a solution: a drug, an operation, some treatment that will make us better. But, for some of these long-term conditions, it is about acceptance that this just may not be an option. This can be extremely difficult to accept, especially for a young student just beginning their life out in the world. But, in reality, it is one of the most difficult things for anybody to accept.

It can help anyone with a long-term disability to build a heightened awareness of their relationship with their body. This is a bit like making a 'pact' with their body. In this situation it is vital for them to listen to their body, to really pay attention to what their body most needs. There may be times when their body needs rest, and they might be ignoring this and doing too much. There may be times when their body needs more exercise, more stimulation. It is important for such clients to build trust in their relationship with their body and become as sensitive as they can to what their body needs at different times. For all of us, our ability to listen to and learn from our bodies is an important way to achieve a healthy balance.

In addition, there is the pain of dealing with other people's expectations, well-meaning family and friends, who can be embarrassed or think that it is helpful to be positive about the possibilities of a potential cure or a treatment. Many people find it hard to believe or accept that there are lifelong conditions that may simply need to be lived with, despite the pain of that.

A disease like Parkinson's, at the moment, has no 'cure' and then it is essential to accept that it may gradually get worse and worse over an unknown period of time, which is very hard for the individual suffering from it, but it is also extremely hard for any partner, family and friends. It is valuable for the sufferer themselves, but also for their partners to be able to access counselling or other support. It is a huge loss and stress for both people in this relationship as they are both living with this debilitating disease on a day-to-day level. It is important to take account too of any children still living in the family home and other family members who may be very involved in any necessary day-to-day care. Sometimes, the clients themselves, are able to achieve a certain level of acceptance, but it doesn't mean that this is without times of the deepest pain, fear, anguish, anger, despair or sadness for them and for their family. It is important to get support to develop new ways of doing things. It is also important to focus on what you can do, as well as knowing when you need support.

Trust What You Know

What would seem to be helpful in the counselling is to help our clients acknowledge that although there may well be periods that are better and easier, they may not last. It would be valuable then to ask them what they have found most helpful, if anything, during these most difficult times. Is it important to learn to accept that they may not get better in the long term? It is helpful to encourage them to think positively and to acknowledge that they will have periods when their abilities and energy may flow more easily. Most clients who have a history of Parkinson's will know already what helps them and what often just makes it worse. They are, after all, the experts on themselves and it is important to encourage them to take control of what they have discovered does help them.

Sometimes, doing creative things such as painting, drawing, writing, handicrafts, sculpture, whatever is of most interest, can change the focus enough to be able to feel able to take back control in a positive way for periods of time. There is such satisfaction in creativity that can inspire us and bring us joy.

It will be important for these clients to discuss their various conditions with their tutors, including discussions of what is possible for them and what is most difficult. It needs to be important to create more flexibility, to put into place any help and support they will need. To take breaks in study, longer deadlines, more access to tutors. Help with physical access to lecture theatres, seminar room, loos and social areas. There needs to be a commitment to be able to put into place anything that will help them to continue on their courses. They will especially need suitable access to academic staff, medical and ancillary medical services, the counselling service and anything that would result in their being able to continue on their course and achieve their degree in the easiest possible way.

Case Story of Cathy – Coping with ME

Cathy was a second-year student studying English and Creative writing. She came for counselling because she felt she really needed more support for her long-term ME It had been difficult enough for her to finally get this diagnosis, as a teenager. This was only after years of her parents taking her to different doctors, who tried all sorts of tests and made suggestions that turned out to be irrelevant.

She had eventually seen a new GP at her home medical centre, who specialised in debilitating, chronic illnesses, and she had immediately realised that Cathy had ME. Her symptoms fitted and since then, Cathy had been able to adjust to her lapses in energy, which can sometimes be extremely debilitating. This same GP in her home town had set up a very helpful group she was able to go to which brought together several young people with similar long-term illnesses. It had been harder for her here at university, since there was no such group available, but she did keep in touch with some people from the group in her home town.

Cathy had decided to come for counselling, just to feel there was some support for her on campus, somewhere she could go and just let off steam or be sad, and it was okay. I asked her to tell me what it was like for her on a day-to-day basis.

"Just that some days it feels like everything is just more difficult. I'm used to the energy lapses, suddenly feeling 'empty' of energy, but sometimes I just feel, why me, why now, when I'm a student". "Sometimes I'm just tired of being tired". "I'm angry with being angry, when people forget or just don't understand what it's like". I asked her, "What helps?" "Well, I've always loved reading and that magical world in books. I get really involved in that sense of a different place, interesting characters, who can do anything! I get to feel as if I am living a different, fuller life, inside a book, a play, a world that can be anything I want it to be". "I suppose in some ways, it is an escape, but, when I write it is great to feel in control of creating my own scenarios, stories, characters. This is something I can do well".

Sometimes, even her love of reading and discussing books didn't help. Suddenly, it was as if she just had nothing to offer, no energy, as if the very life in her just dimmed, and she just had to go and rest. She had felt like this most of her life, and she knew the signs in her body; she knew what she needed. During those times, she just couldn't join in with her friends here on campus, because she was suddenly exhausted and just had to go and rest. It was hard to always have to explain to other people and see them occasionally, just not understand, or maybe think she was being a bit of a wimp. Some fellow students were sympathetic, but she could see that some were impatient, disinterested and just had no idea.

She had learnt to accept most of that, but there were times, when she felt angry, impatient with her body.

Her family had been very supportive when they eventually discovered that she had ME, and having found a doctor who knew about it at home, had really helped.

What was difficult sometimes was that she would really be excited about, what she was reading, what she was writing. Then, as if from nowhere, it was as if all the life in her drained away. She had to stop what she was excited about. She was learning even now how to accept this, and sometimes, it seemed so unfair.

From being in the group in her home town, Cathy knew exactly what she could do that would help her, breathing exercises, meditation, good diet, and she was very good at taking care of herself, but she sometimes needed to use the counselling just to 'let off steam', to come to terms with feelings of 'unfairness'. She didn't come along for counselling weekly. She would make an appointment when she really needed it.

She occasionally found it useful to draw colourful pictures of herself, her mood, how her body felt, and how she felt about her body. Occasionally, she would just sit and cry, feeling that loss in her of the vitality she saw and sometimes envied in her friends, especially the fact that they often just took that for granted. Sometimes she would alternate between feeling 'pissed off' and 'crying out the frustration and the sadness' – it was a release for her. Also, there were times when she was really great at 'bouncing back' and engaging with her love of studying English.

What I saw grow in Cathy was a mature and real acceptance of her illness, the self-knowledge that she had developed to know what would help in most situations she found herself in and the joy in her when she could fully engage in her course and friendships on campus. She was an absolute pleasure to work with.

Case Story of Jake – Coping with Parkinson's

Jake was a mature student just beginning in his second and final year of studying for an MA in the History of Art. In the summer holidays, he had been diagnosed with Parkinson's disease, which had been a big shock for him. He was 38, married with two children, a boy of 14 and a girl of 12, both of whom were at a local grammar school. His wife was working as a teacher in a local junior school. His wife had persuaded him to come for counselling.

> "First of all, Jake, I can see from your assessment notes, that you've only just had a diagnosis of Parkinsons Disease, I'm very sorry that you are having to face such a difficult challenge. How would you like to use the counselling?"
>
> "Well, my wife, Judy, first persuaded me to go to the doctors because of my leg and the shakiness, and now she's persuaded me to come along here, just to try and come to terms with what feels like a massive, 'train' speeding towards me. I don't really know what to say".

"That's a pretty scary description".

Jake's eyes welled up and he breathed out really hard.

"I never thought something like this would happen to me, not now, not ever. I'm afraid for Judy, for Carol for Trevor and for myself. I just want to be there for them. Sorry to cry".

"That's totally understandable Jake, this is a big thing for you to take in".

"Too right!"

He took some deep breaths and blew his nose a couple of times, but this was hard for him. I gave him some space.

"The worst bit is the idea of being a burden to my family, but worse still is just not being there for Carol and Trevor. I couldn't bear putting them through all of this".

"How much do you know about Parkinsons?"

"Well, I've read the stuff the doctor gave me. I guess, I'm still taking it in. They've given me the number of a local group, that would be good for me to contact. I just can't do that yet".

"That's understandable, you need to take it in first. But when you are ready it would be good to get more information from other people who are actually going through this, that is a good support for you. It's great that you came along for some counselling too".

"I honestly can't believe this is happening, I'm only 38, it seems so young for something like this. The doctor said, it's still in the early stages. It began with occasional tremors and my left leg had stiffened up for no apparent reason. Also, I just felt anxious, really felt anxious today about coming here".

"Was it as bad as you imagined?"

"No, well only facing up to this whole thing, it's actually been easier than I thought it would be. I'm thinking of joining the local group, just that I suppose, we'd all be in it together".

"That's a really good idea and each of you may have found things that help and can share that. You may find other students there as well"

"Well actually someone on the MA has already given me the number of a friend of his who lives locally and was diagnosed a couple of years ago".

"That's great Jake, you've been really very proactive to reach out".

"Well, I reckon if anyone who's in the same position knows things that will help, well, that's a good thing".

"It really is".

"I'm lucky Judy is very supportive and she believes in getting advice as soon as possible, I would have probably left it. She's right. I'm glad I came here to talk about it".

Jake came back for one more session, more of a check-in, a month later, to say that he had now been to the Parkinson's local group and there was another mature student in the group. It was really helpful for him to be in a group of people who were in a similar situation. Some of them had been in the group for many years, which he saw as optimistic!

It felt less scary, and he realised he was more or less at the beginning of what would be a long journey, an unknown journey, who knows what cures there may be in the future. He sounded positive but also accepting that this was not an easy path to be on. He also felt totally supported by his wife, family and friends, which all helped.

At the end of the session, I just confirmed with Jake that any time he felt he needed to, he could set up a counselling session. This felt for him like another support he could turn to when he needed it. He was actually coping really well considering it was a relatively new diagnosis but it sounded as if he had really good support from his wife.

Chapter 9

Domestic Abuse – When Charm Turns to Harm

Living with Domestic Abuse

It can take a lot of courage for a client to come for counselling if they are being abused at home. It is usually the sign of a positive step, of acceptance on their part, that something is badly wrong. The decision to get help is a positive step forward, towards them getting other support they may need, which may involve being re-housed on campus, as well as ongoing counselling.

Although I've witnessed some people be able to work to change their relationships for the better, even if it has become abusive to one or both partners, it can also be valuable to seek help to leave a relationship. Sometimes, it is helpful in ongoing counselling to discuss what might be possible to salvage and what might not be. Often, people stay in an abusive relationship for too long. It is hard to accept that we are being abused by a partner, because then there is the obvious question that follows, "what do we need to do about it?".

Sometimes, people blame themselves for doing something wrong. There are situations where people may have grown up with abusive parents and have almost come to accept abuse as being a 'normal' way of behaving in relationships.

It can be difficult if there are children involved, because the partner being abused may not want to deprive their children of the other parent. It may be difficult financially to leave if there is nowhere affordable or suitable that is available. This may also lead to them seeking help on campus for temporary accommodation.

I have often worked with women and men who blame themselves for the violence in their partner, sometimes because the partner has also blamed them for their own violence, rather than acknowledge that they have a problem. When emotions are mixed up, disturbed by anger, fear, anxiety about an unknown future, feeling unsafe or insecure, for all kinds of reasons, it can be extremely hard for anyone to acknowledge that they are being abused or that they are being abusive. There is often a lot of denial in such relationships.

It is an important step for anyone to seek counselling for domestic abuse. It is certainly an acknowledgement on behalf of the person seeking help, that they want to change what is happening, which is most often a positive step forward. It may also lead to them seeking help on campus for temporary accommodation.

DOI: 10.4324/9781003754244-11

It can be that a student who is living at home with abusive parents can come along for counselling to find a way of leaving the family home, which again, may need a referral to the accommodation office for them to be re-housed on campus if necessary. It may be that someone is living in student accommodation where they feel threatened by a housemate, who is being abusive to them or to another housemate. Again, this may involve a need to find new accommodation for the student wanting to leave, or some kind of disciplinary action to remove the person causing the problem.

Case Story of Anita – Domestic Abuse

Anita had been booked into an emergency assessment slot for counselling. She was very distressed and had a plaster cast on her arm. She was in tears, and I suggested she just take a few minutes to relax as much as she could and take some deep breaths in and out. She took some time and gradually relaxed. She apologised for being 'in a state'. I reassured her. She was obviously very upset.

"I've left my husband, not before time. He did this at the weekend", she was pointing to her arm in plaster. "Darren just lost it and hit me with a heavy saucepan from the draining board. He stormed off, no doubt to the pub". "One of our neighbours took my son, Terry, and me, to the hospital". "I phoned my dad from the hospital and he came to get Terry and me, later that evening". "My dad drove us back to the house, so we could pack some cases with clothes and other things, fortunately Darren was not around". "I can't go back there again, while he is there. Luckily, we can stay with my mum and dad for a week or two, but they are about 40 miles away from Terry's school and the university".

I asked if anything like this had happened before. She told me nothing as serious as this had happened before, but he had threatened me a few times in the last few months. "He has had problems at work and he's become increasingly angry a lot of the time, with me and with our son Terry. Darren has begun to resent me being here at university".

> "I've booked in to see a solicitor, later this week to see what my options are in terms of safeguarding for Terry and the chances of a temporary separation or anything I can do to get him out of the house".

"Otherwise, I will need to find alternative accommodation locally here for Terry to get to his school and for me to continue with my course on campus".

> "It's such a mess and needs sorting out. I know now that I don't want to go back. He's never been violent before but, his drinking has become a bigger and bigger problem. I need to get Terry and myself away from him".

I asked if she thought Darren would consider getting any help for his alcohol problems. She had suggested it, but he just got angry. "He just doesn't acknowledge that he has a problem". "I'm sorry, that must be very difficult for you and for Terry".

Anita made an appointment for a full counselling session the following week. She said she would email Darren to ask if he would be willing to accept some help and maybe move in with his parents for a bit so that she and Terry could stay in the house local to the university and Terry's school.

Anita came back for counselling the following week. She looked quite a bit calmer. Darren had begrudgingly moved out of their house and had moved in with his parents, who lived about 10 miles away. His parents had been quite shocked by what had happened, especially the injury to Anita. They were urging Darren to get help for his alcohol problem. They actually found details of a therapist who specialised in alcohol related problems. They had a good relationship with Terry, so they were happy to be around if Terry went to see Darren at their house. Luckily Anita got on pretty well with her in-laws.

It had been a positive step that Darren had been willing to move out of their marital home. Both Darren and Anita got good support from both of their sets of parents, which really helped the whole situation. Anita continued with counselling for several weeks and had an occasional counselling appointment monthly for some time, which she found very helpful. Darren also, eventually, admitted to having a growing alcohol problem and was willing to see the therapist that his parents had found. They both decided to live separately until Anita had finished her degree, which would take just over a year to complete. Darren did some extra training for his work, which increased his self-esteem. They eventually began to meet up regularly as a couple and doing things together with Terry. They took their time but seemed to have a strong commitment to make this relationship work.

Chapter 10

Eating Disorders – Balancing the Bread

What Stops the Joy of Eating?

What gets in the way of our joy of eating is often what gets in the way of our joy of living. Some of that can be pressure from outside of us to achieve perfection. There can be enormous expectations on women and men to have, to be, to achieve, more and more in every area of our lives. There are so many messages and images in advertising, in the media, in our working lives, compelling us to look perfect, to perform, to possess, to be successful in every avenue of life. Often this leaves less time for genuine relaxation and play with friends, family or with ourselves. There is pressure to achieve rather than time to relax, have fun and be in the moment. We all need time for sitting quietly, really being 'with' ourselves or with the landscape around us, appreciating and enjoying ourselves for who we are. We need to take time out to bring ourselves into balance, to find what gives us real joy.

Some addictive behaviours, particularly around food and eating, stem from unresolved past or present traumas. We can also experience a deep 'hunger' caused by past or present deprivation, unfilled desires, or a deep tiredness caused by just too much pressure and stress. Any addictive behaviour, especially around food and eating, that helps us to feel temporarily 'full up and satisfied', can then quickly cause us to experience a 'running away from ourselves' into self-blame, low self-esteem and often a damaging emotional void. This potential vicious circle is a poor substitute for our basic need to connect with our True Selves.

To find a way back to respect for our True Selves, it is helpful for us to begin to positively support ourselves in the way we think about ourselves and in the way we talk to ourselves, the best we can. For us to feel good about ourselves, to find a balance in our lives, to grow a sense of peace, we do need to forgive ourselves for being just who we are. We all make mistakes; that's how we learn. Forgiveness is a part of self-love and self-acceptance that we need to be fully where we are now. This creates an inner joy in ourselves. This is the healthiest way to boost and heal the part of us that may have experienced past trauma, deprivation, or may have experienced, as a defence, that it is better not to feel anything at all.

Most people experiencing any over-consuming or addictions have usually learned to be adept at blaming themselves. The truth is that at least some of the

DOI: 10.4324/9781003754244-12

problem is that we are manipulated by companies, making huge amounts of money from producing highly addictive substances, that they relentlessly promote, so that many of us can choose to run away from ourselves and then most unfairly blame ourselves for this.

Then, for any of us who want to 'lose weight', there is an enormous industry, producing 'slimming products', many of which don't seem to work in the long term. These companies also make huge profits at the expense of people who are often disappointed in the products and more importantly in themselves. There is a lot of evidence that most weight is gained within a year of attempting to lose it. I have worked with many clients whose problems with eating began with 'dieting'.

The hardest thing with eating disorders is that so many people blame themselves, hate themselves for their perceived 'weakness'. This lowers self-esteem and can cause us to increase our need to 'run away from ourselves', which I believe is one of the most important reasons for over-eating, any addiction really. So, it really can easily become 'a vicious circle'. The more someone disappears into an eating disorder, the more they punish themselves and the more they disappear into the eating disorder. So, in counselling, it is important to recognise this process and encourage our clients to find a way out, a way to forgive themselves, connect with themselves more, in a positive way, and give themselves alternatives to their over-eating. They need support and information, as well as finding ways to increase their self-esteem and build a positive relationship with themselves, so that they can be really present and accepting of themselves enough to make healthier choices for themselves.

As a student counsellor, I would hear so many young people express feelings of inadequacy at not being perfect in every way. This was particularly prevalent in young people who were desperately afraid of putting on weight. Students who set themselves standards that were unrealistic and lived with feelings of self-hatred when they couldn't reach this level of perfection. It felt as if they were living in a painful prison of bullying expectations. It helped them to be able to identify that 'bully' in themselves. Sometimes it really helped for clients, as homework, to draw or paint a picture of that 'bully'. Many clients had not realised just how hard they were being on themselves. Most of these students knew exactly what 'the bully' would look like, and most were horrified by what they had drawn. It really helped them to understand how disrespectful they felt towards themselves. One client made a clay model of 'that voice'. It was so mean-looking that she could now laugh at it. This took away the power of it to berate her. Some clients realised in their counselling that, 'that voice', had been coming from someone in their family or circle, who had been bullying them or expecting too much of them.

This was followed up by some clients being willing to create an image of something that represented a much kinder voice they could develop inside themselves, as a real support.

On occasions, it was useful for the client to do a role-play of both themselves in one chair and with the bully within them sitting in another chair in the room. This was a helpful way for the client to see clearly what they were doing to themselves. Again, as with the clay model, some clients could almost laugh at just how awful, 'the bully within', had been towards them.

When counselling, I kept a note on the wall of my counselling room with 70% on it. This would remind me and remind some clients that aiming to do something 70% well is really good, especially when we are learning something new or testing out any new behaviour. When we exercise our muscles or 'work out', 70% would easily stretch our muscles in a positive way that helps us to develop fitness. Over that, it can tip us into straining ourselves. So often we have expectations of ourselves that we need to achieve 100% in all sorts of ways in our lives. This is mostly an unrealistic goal and in physical achievements could be likely to result in an injury, unless you are a good amateur or professional athlete. The truth is that as humans we are perfect in our imperfection. Our variety and difference is the most individual and wonderful thing about us. Can you imagine going into a forest and saying, "That tree really is too fat"; "That tree is the wrong colour and texture"; "That tree is an awkward shape on one side". It would be ridiculous because each tree is unique and beautiful as it is, and this is no less true for human beings.

Anorexia as a Symbol of Success Can Become a Prison

Anorexia is an addictive behaviour that is based on an extreme fear of being overweight. It causes people to take in far too little food and taken to extremes it can be life-threatening. Behind anorexia is often a goal of perfection. Rather than being 'good enough' or 'doing our best' there is an unachievable level of perfection just in front of us and a sense of, "if only I could be……I'd be okay/acceptable/loveable". Often someone with anorexia sees themselves as overweight when they are often seriously underweight. This distortion can be overwhelming. This aiming for some kind of perfection can result in some people being dramatically and unhealthily underweight.

Anorexia is most common in young women but men can also suffer from Anorexia and it is most prevalent in the mid-teens but is experienced by all ages. Anorexia often leads to avoiding food, but also can lead to us avoiding eating with other people; missing out on sociable meals or simply eating the smallest amounts, sometimes cut up into small pieces. Someone who is anorexic will eat either very fast or excessively slow and they often lie to family or friends about having eaten when they haven't. They quite often exercise excessively and will lie about their weight, which is most often, unhealthily low. Some people with anorexia wear baggy clothes to disguise their bodies. They mostly don't like being out of control and are sensitive about being judged by others. Meal times can be stressful, and there can also be a preoccupation with calorie counting and exercise.

People who are anorexic are often introverts and can experience personality traits such as perfectionism or Obsessive Compulsive Disorder. They can often experience anxiety or depression. Partly due to lack of food, they can sometimes find it hard to concentrate and think clearly.

Anorexia – Not Wanting to Grow Up?

Another cause of Anorexia that can be prevalent is a sense of not wanting to become an adult woman or man. In fact, wanting to stay a child and, sometimes, not wanting to be in a sexual relationship. Commonly, there can be a power struggle in the home of someone who has anorexia. Of course, this would often be about food or eating, with one or both parents. Sometimes, not eating can be a way of exerting power, in the distress it causes to other family members, or even in friendship groups.

Historically, there was a huge societal change in the UK when 'Twiggy' became 'The Face of 1966', the top fashion model, an example of what was the new desirable model and new 'standard' for what young women needed to achieve, a perfect 'girl' size body, even somewhat androgenous, at the time. Breasts were frowned upon, and it felt like womanhood changed overnight to reflect an image of something that was rather derogatory of most women at that time.

Over that period of time, the slimming industry became worth millions, even billions of pounds. However, it was a fad of fashion, that damaged men and women's self-esteem and created pressure, particularly for women, to look more like, 'girls'. The whole 'diet' industry made food something that many people became 'afraid of'. I believe this 'era' was an important part of the cause of the proliferation of eating disorders.

Also, having worked with so many adults, abused as children, I often wonder if this whole era encouraged a proliferation in the sexualisation of 'girls' and 'boys', on a massive scale.

Case Story of Anna – Anorexia

Anna has a quiet voice, a lovely lilting Scottish accent, which made me smile. She sat, hardly taking up any space in her chair. She had lovely long brown hair, big brown eyes and a quiet smile. I could see that she was noticeably underweight. I knew from her assessment notes that she was coming for counselling because of anorexia, which she's experienced for three years, since going into the sixth form at school. She had a year out after school to travel and work in France and is now a first-year student studying law. Her anorexia had been quite severe during her sixth form, but improved when she was away in France. She has come now because it's all started up again since coming to university.

I asked her how she was settling in on campus and what she wanted to get out of the counselling. She smiled shyly and told me she had good housemates and felt good about finally beginning at university. She'd enjoyed her year in France, but she was finding it difficult not to get pulled into her old pattern of anorexia. Some of those old feelings had come back. I asked her to tell me a bit about what her feelings were. She became tearful.

"It was a bit better in France, I was staying on a farm owned by relations of my mum, doing some work experience in exchange for staying there. We'd often visited them when I was a child and I was outside a lot and felt freer, not so much pressure. I enjoy speaking French, which I grew up speaking. The people on the farm are lovely and I have always felt safe there". "You know from the other counsellor that I didn't always feel safe at home before that".

"Yes, it sounded from your assessment that it was tough for you at home. What was it like when you got back from France".

"I found the strength to deal with my dad and I finally told my mum about his sexual abuse of me. I especially wanted to protect my sister who is five years younger than me". "I want to be sure he doesn't start all of that with her".

"After it started with my dad, my brother once saw him leaving my bedroom and found me in tears" "He'd asked me a few times if there was a problem with dad, but he didn't know exactly what was going on". "I didn't tell him the full story until this summer". "He was away at uni. most of that time, when it was happening". When I did speak to him, it helped him to talk to a good friend of his who had been through something similar in his extended family.

"My mum threw my dad out of the house and threatened to go to the police if he set foot in the house again.

She is furious with him and is divorcing him". "I feel relieved for my sister's sake". "I really hate him, but I'm not afraid of him anymore". I just don't want to ever see him or have anything to do with him again".

"Tell me about the anorexia", I asked her. "I think I just wanted to 'disappear'. I wanted my body to disappear". "I hated my body". "I think I thought if I stopped eating, he wouldn't be interested in me in that way". "I just wanted it to stop". "I couldn't tell my mum or anyone else, I didn't want to hurt her". "I got used to hiding in clothes that were too big for me, but my mum kept asking why I wasn't eating properly".

"It was a relief to get here, to university and I love my course, I love doing law. I feel like I can do something to help others".

"The problem is, I still feel revolted by eating". "I know I'm underweight but I still want to be invisible".

"I don't know how to get out of this habit of not wanting to eat". "I think I'm blaming my body for what he did to me".

I asked her what would help her now – what does she need from all of this that has happened to her.

She sat in her chair, hands on her head, leaning back, looking upwards for answers for a few minutes.

"For now, I know I don't want anything to do with him again. I think I need to tell him what I think and feel, just get it out of me".

I asked if it might help her to write a letter to him and maybe put an empty chair out in the counselling room and read it to him.

Anna was thoughtful, "Yes, I think that would help".

I asked Anna what she felt her body needed. She decided that she would seek out a massage therapist, a woman, and just see if that can help me find pleasure in my body again. I feel like I need to fight to get it back, but maybe a gentle massage would bring peace to my body.

We made an appointment for two weeks on.

Anna came in the door, looking less pale. She had bought the letter she wanted to read out to an empty chair, which represented her father. She had already found a really good massage therapist who was very experienced at working with people who had experienced trauma. She had been for one session and was booked in for a series of five more. She felt she had chosen, just the right person and it was very therapeutic for her.

I was so impressed with her determination to 'get well', 'to let go of the past', 'to get her whole self, back again'.

She read out the letter to her father, 'in the empty chair'. It was a very powerful letter, and she didn't completely close the door to her father. She asked that he go and get therapeutic help, not just for her sake but especially for the sake of her little sister. She told him that right now she didn't want to see him again but maybe she would feel differently, if he got real help for his problem of being an abuser. She then decided to send it to him.

Anna had several further sessions, specifically about the anorexia. She realised that the anorexia really was about wanting her body/herself to 'disappear'. It was very hard for her to break the habit of not wanting to eat and when she put on a few pounds, she was scared. She was willing to do a regular breathing meditation, which did help her anxiety and shakiness, which was sometimes a problem, when she was afraid of eating too much.

Bulimia, a Distressing Way of Numbing Out and Self-Harming

Bulimia is an eating disorder that causes people to constantly worry about eating or being overweight, who then go on to develop a distorted and negative body image. There is a pattern of eating excessively, in one sitting, usually not around other people. They will then retreat to the bathroom, very soon after eating, and make themselves vomit. This nearly always happens in secret. Sometimes this same person will take part in excessive fasting or excessive exercise as well.

This behaviour often creates either a normal or slightly above-average body weight. This behaviour is usually based on a fear of being out of control, a fear of not being able to stop eating and a fear of putting on weight. Sometimes, bulimia also includes a misuse of laxatives or diuretics.

The overriding presenting problem from a bulimic client in the counselling room is an abusive relationship with eating and eliminating food from their body, which amounts to an abusive relationship with their body. A bulimic client can also experience severe problems with unhealthy teeth due to excess stomach acid damaging the enamel of their teeth. A bulimic client who makes themselves excessively sick may also be suffering from malnutrition and anaemia, bowel problems including constipation and damage of the inner lining of the throat, caused by excess stomach acid. Other complications with clients suffering from bulimia can be irregular or absent periods.

Bulimia nervosa can become a learnt behaviour, from the pressures in society to have 'a perfect figure' or may be a learnt behaviour that is prevalent in the client's friends or family. It can be as a result of low self-esteem, particularly in relation to body image. It may simply be a combination of all of these things. It is a serious eating disorder and as such a serious mental illness.

If this becomes a chronic condition, it can often last from 5 to 10 years and usually at least 50% of women recover from this disorder, but some go on with symptoms for quite a lot longer, particularly if they don't seek help. Bulimia is best treated by a team of therapists, dietitians and doctors. It is often treated with CBT, other individual therapy, family therapy or group therapy. Antidepressants can often help to decrease the compulsion to binge eat and vomit.

The excessive vomiting and use of laxatives associated with bulimia can lead to an electrolyte imbalance that raises the risk for abnormal heart rhythms. This damage to the heart can eventually lead to congestive heart failure. This eating disorder can harm a client's psychological well-being in many different ways, including anxiety, lack of concentration, mood swings, depression, a lack of motivation and a lack of engagement in life generally, some impaired comprehension, a decreased ability in problem solving.

Both of these above eating disorders tend to become prevalent from about 12 years old to the mid-twenties, mostly in girls and young women but this also affects about 10% of young men.

In bulimic clients there can be a history of childhood abuse, emotional abuse particularly. They may have experienced in their family a problem with secrecy and isolation, denial of problems. It is good to ask them to assess what is likely to cause a relapse in them.

It is good to discuss with these clients what they feel might get them back into control. It is helpful to encourage them to take responsibility for themselves, e.g. planning meals and snacks that are healthy; asking them to work out what the triggers are for the binge eating; asking them what would help them change and manage their negative feelings about themselves and their body image. It is important to encourage them to focus on what they think works to get them back into balance and healthier habits. This is all part of them beginning to build a healthier inner relationship with themselves.

Case Story of Caroline – Bulimia

Caroline was a second-year student who was studying biochemistry. She was referred by a housemate who knew she was often very unwell. I felt she really didn't want to be here. She shifted around in her seat and seemed very uncomfortable. She had difficulty looking me in the face; she looked around in the room as she spoke.

"Well, my housemate suggested that I should come along. I am often not well and she is worried about me, that there might be something seriously wrong with me".

I asked her why she had come to the counselling service rather than the G.P. She again shifted around in her seat and looked as if she just wanted to get up and run away.

"Well, I think it might be a psychological condition rather than a medical one".

I asked her to tell me a little more. She looked a bit disgruntled, not really wanting to be here.

"Well, I do have a problem with making myself sick. It's been around for quite some time and maybe it really is time I talk to someone"

"What kinds of things make you feel like doing this Caroline".

"Well, I suppose I'm very afraid of being overweight and this behaviour helps me to keep my weight down. I do have a real problem with eating too much. I've tried various diets, but none of them really work. I then discovered that the best thing was to just make myself sick. It would stop me being overweight. I suppose I'm a bit ashamed to admit to this, it does seem a very odd thing to do. I've just got used to doing it since I was a teenager".

"Have you sought any help for this before"

"No, I suppose I feel a bit ashamed of what I am doing".

"I'm sorry that you feel like that. It is a really good thing that you are now seeking help. It takes a lot of courage to talk about these things. Have you developed any symptoms that might be of concern from doing this?"

"I know I have problems with my teeth and I kind of avoid going to the dentist. I know that's not a good thing to do".

"Would you be prepared to get a check-up?"

"I know I need to and well, coming here is part of me admitting to myself that I need help, so maybe I can do that too".

"That's really good. You don't need to cope with this on your own. We are used to helping people with this, particularly on campus. It might be good if you had a check-up with your dentist here".

"I've just been ignoring it for years. It used to feel like a relief, a way out of the pressures I was feeling but now I'm thinking it has become a problem in itself".

"I think it's really good that you have come to seek help and that is often the most difficult step to take. Well done for that. We are lucky on campus to have a medical centre that has a psychotherapist that specialises in working with people with eating disorders. I am thinking it would be good for you to see her. She sees people individually initially but she also runs a group for people with eating problems. Would you consider seeing her, first for some individual sessions, and then maybe joining the group?"

"Well, I didn't know about that. I think that it has gone on for so long, it makes sense to see someone who can offer something longer term and more specialised. I didn't know that was on offer for students".

"I am happy to do a referral letter to her. What do you think would be useful for her to know?"

"Well, I guess I began this when I was about 14. My parents were quite critical of me putting on weight as a teenager, they would never do that, they are both very slim, exercise a lot, go running, are sporty. I'm just not like that. They have always had high expectations of me and my brother. He's very clever, like them, and I guess I felt a bit, the odd one out".

"They are all three very successful. I like science, particularly biochemistry, but I don't love it. I'm enjoying my course and doing okay but, I'm not sure it's for me. I sometimes think that I'm living this life for someone else, not for me. Does that sound weird?"

"Not at all, what do you think you would really want for yourself?"

"Well for a start, no-one has every really asked me that?"

"What I enjoy most is being around animals, they don't judge you, I've always loved animals. I wanted to work on a farm in the summer, near us at home, but both of my parents discouraged me, felt it was a waste of time, didn't pay much".

"Could you find some part-time work around here, as a weekend job?"

"I've not thought about it, I know I would enjoy that contact with animals. I used to help out on a friend's farm at home occasionally, but my parents were rather derogatory about it".

"You look enthusiastic when you talk about that".

Caroline smiled for the first time.

"How would you feel about a referral to the medical centre? It does sound as if you would benefit from some slightly longer-term help".

"I think that sounds good. I do really want to sort this out".

"I'll do a referral letter and they will be in touch with you very soon. I'm very glad you sound so positive about getting the help you need".

In one of our regular meetings with the medical centre staff, I heard that Caroline was doing really well from the help she was having.

Binge Eating to Fill the Emptiness Inside

Binge eating, like other eating disorders, is again, a way of 'running away from our inner selves', including running away from our thoughts and feelings. Our clients are the experts on themselves, and therefore, it is important to encourage them to take responsibility for discovering what the triggers are for binging. It can help to encourage them to make a list of what thoughts and feelings trigger their binging. It could be feelings of frustration, being tired, tense, low self-esteem, anxiety, stress, pressure, boredom, anger, something missing, needing a break, feeling overwhelmed or having negative feelings about themselves caused by this behaviour. It is important to encourage these clients to build self-awareness to build a real connection and good understanding of themselves and their behaviour and if possible, forgiveness for themselves rather than self-punishment. It can be really hard to be stuck in compulsive behaviour that really doesn't feel like a choice.

It can be that past or present trauma in a client's life has contributed to the need to binge eat? It is important to check out with them how long binge eating has been a coping mechanism and if they have an awareness of what might have caused the start of this behaviour. It is important to check out if there is anyone else in their family who shares difficulties with food or eating?

What have they found to be helpful in stopping them from binging? What does it feel like when they first get that feeling of wanting to binge? Can they take a few moments to find a distraction or an intervention that might work to stop themselves binging? Would it help them to drink water or eat a favourite piece of fruit to feel full up in a good way? Would it be helpful for them to contact someone, just for a chat? Would any music they enjoy be a distraction? Would it help them to get up and move, go for a walk or run?

Longer term, is there anything they would like to get involved with on campus? Anything that would build their self-esteem, distract them: painting, drawing, playing music, exercise, playing games, volunteering, playing sport, more social contact, anything, they might have always wanted to try.

Longer term, do they need to build a better relationship with food, having food available that they really enjoy, that is really healthy and good for them? Even cooking special dishes they enjoy, to keep in a freezer, so that there is always something there that they like. Would it help them to have more meals with friends? How could food become nourishing for them again, so that it is not the enemy?

Building a healthier, more positive relationship with themselves is important. So again, their being able to forgive themselves is important. Thinking about what they feel 'empty' of. Is there anything they feel they need or want, in terms of activities, contact with people, more stimulation, more rest and relaxation. Can they imagine what might fill that 'emptiness' for them? Did the food really help? What else can they imagine might help? Can they think of any patterns in their family, anything at home that increased their need to overeat? What has helped them in the past to break any habits, patterns or behaviour? Can they be gentle with themselves? Can they help themself? If not, what would block them from doing that? Can they draw a picture of the block?

Can they make a real effort to get back a good relationship with their body, or with themselves generally? What would be good to do for themselves? Could they exchange a foot massage with a housemate? Could they join a club or activity group, a yoga or meditation class? Buy themselves something great to wear? Buy something special for their room? What would they most appreciate as a gift or a treat from themselves?

What do they know that might help them not to binge? Does it help to eat more slowly? Can they differentiate when they are really hungry or when they are eating for some other reason: a feeling of boredom, a need for water, to fill an emptiness within, to calm a feeling of anxiety or some other reason. It is good for them to stop and think about this, even keep a list of different reasons why they binge eat. Would it help them instead to move around, to go for a walk, to sit and do some breathing exercises, again, phone a friend. It can only help them to get to know themselves and their needs better. Self-awareness really helps to change behaviour. It's just about getting to know and care for ourselves better. We deserve it!

We Can All Make Different Choices

What really helps us to change, make different choices, is first of all, being a real friend to ourselves. If it was your best friend who'd made a mistake, eaten too much, felt bad about herself or himself, would you then be angry with them? or be disappointed in them? If they really were your friend, you'd understand, realise they need a bit of help, be kind to them, forgive them. Maybe you'd persuade them, they can do better next time. They are worth giving another chance to, and so are you.

We can all get into patterns that are harmful; we can all get it wrong, whatever it is. That's when we need most encouragement to give ourselves another chance. I think one of the main difficulties with eating disorders is that we are so hard on ourselves and that really doesn't help us. Of course we want to help ourselves be healthier, but we can more easily make different choices from a place of higher self-esteem, forgiveness, generosity and kindness to ourselves.

I think that we live in a world that really pushes us very hard to spend money on products that are often harmful for us. So much of our food is laden with addictive salt, sugar and probably other additives we know little about. It is not always easy to resist those kinds of food, that we've been strongly persuaded to be comforted by. We need to give ourselves some support if we have got into unhealthy habits, to help ourselves really be genuinely kinder to ourselves. Then, I think it will be just that bit easier for us to make healthier, more sensible choices for ourselves.

Most people respond so much better to kindness, generosity and positivity, so it is really important that we begin making better choices in the ways we think of ourselves, speak to ourselves and encourage ourselves, if we want to change our actions towards ourselves. I believe we can increase our joy by just making more conscious choices. This is how we take charge of our lives. This is how we change our lives.

I believe that what we focus on, grows. If we focus on what's wrong rather than what's right then that is often where our energy goes. As human beings I believe we have the capacity for great negativity and great positivity but what is fantastic and amazing about us is the power that we have to choose…and to change. Some of us don't remember that we have a choice or take the time to choose. Conscious choosing and the anticipation of believing your needs will be met is really living. We deserve the best!

Case Story of Robert – Binge Eating

Robert is a first-year American student. At his assessment, he described finding it hard to settle into university life. It's his first term. He's living in a lively corridor on campus, and he's made one or two friends, but he's missing home. His father is American, and his mother is English, and he has family living in the UK, quite near this university, whom he's been visiting during the summer. He is studying English and has always wanted to come to the UK to study. He didn't think it would be quite so 'different'. Although people are kind and polite, he sort of feels a bit alienated as so many people here don't like Trump. He doesn't either, but he feels a bit embarrassed to be American.

Robert was a good baseball player at home and also grew up playing cricket in a local team in Boston, where his family live. He has joined a university cricket team and is practising using the nets inside the sports hall. He is really keen to play more cricket here, come the better weather.

Robert decided to come for counselling because he has a history of 'binge eating'. He feels quite mixed up about who he is. He doesn't really get on very well with his father, and it was a bit of a relief to make a new start here. He feels close to his mother and gets on well with her family, who live in the UK.

"From your assessment, it sounds that it has been quite difficult settling in here, which has caused you to get back into old behaviour of 'binge eating'. It is quite stressful to begin a degree far from home. What do you think would help you now?"

"I was excited about studying here, but I seem to have bought old behaviour with me and I'm disappointed in myself. I know its stressful beginning a new course, but I feel I have let myself down".

"Do you think you might be being a bit hard on yourself?"

"That makes me feel that I'm more like my father than I want to be".

"Can you tell me a bit about that Robert".

Robert took some deep breaths and was a little bit tearful. "Sorry".

"You don't have to apologise for having feelings here Robert".

Robert put his head down. "I guess I feel ashamed to be so weak".

"Do you see yourself as weak having sad feelings about being so far from home, in a new situation. That's not an easy situation to be in. Can you give yourself some credit for coming here and wanting to get help for the way you are feeling?"

Robert smiles, "I guess I can".

So, what are the triggers, that you recognise for 'binge eating'?

"I think I get really angry with myself and begin to think, why not, it stops me feeling so angry sometimes".

"What have you discovered helps you?"

"Always exercise, walking, running, going to the sports hall".

"That sounds like a good thing to do. Is there anything else that might help too?" "What about writing down how you feel?" "Telling someone else about it?" "Drawing how you feel?" "Any other way of expressing how you feel?"

"It's been a relief to talk to you here, it makes me realise just how hard I've always been on myself. The binging doesn't really work, it just makes me hate myself more, I see that, but I get stuck in a vicious circle".

"It sounds as if you deserve to be a bit kinder to yourself, far from home".

Robert grinned. "I guess there are other ways".

"Are there any friends you've made here who you could talk to about this?"

"Yes, there is one guy, on my corridor, I think would really understand, he got into a circle of self-harming, when he was younger. He found a way out of that, with help from counselling. I have actually told him that I was coming here. I think he would really understand".

"That was brave of you".

"Thank you. Luckily, I don't think I've got too deep into the 'bingeing' yet. I can stop myself sometimes. It has really helped to talk here and kind of face up to it".

"What would be helpful for you, do you want to make another appointment now?"

"I think I've really found today helpful. I'd like to think about it, see what I can change myself. I can talk to one my cousins who lives not far away. She is very easy to talk to. I can also talk to the guy on my corridor.

"I really have appreciated this. I can see why I've felt so uptight. I have been very hard on myself. I want to enjoy my time here. I'd like to try writing down my feelings too. I'd like some time to digest today and come back to you, if I need to. I will let you know. This has been a lot more helpful than bingeing".

We both smiled, and his whole body was less tense, his face more relaxed.

I got an email from Robert, later in the year, to say he had joined the cricket team, was doing well, had made good friends on the team and felt he didn't have to do anything 'perfectly' anymore!!

I think that Robert asking for help had been a big step for him – the ability to be vulnerable. His bingeing had been a warning sign but he hadn't really allowed it to take hold of him. He had been really excited about being here in the UK.

Chapter 11

Exam Strategies and Revision Techniques

Some students find exams really difficult, and it can cause genuine distress. Counselling can sometimes help the student look back at where this deep fear began, and sometimes it is possible to mitigate this fear by the student learning techniques of relaxation, visualisations and meditations. In some extreme situations, it may be possible to get help from the student's academic department to find an alternative to exams in the form of a dissertation. This would depend on agreement with the academic department and the university management.

If this fear is milder, there are two hand-outs that can offer some suggestions, a few Revision Techniques and Exam Strategies that such students might find helpful.

Revision Techniques to Help You Feel in Control

Aim to reduce the bulk of your lecture and reading notes into revision notes that are short, punchy, portable and give pointers to possible answer for exam questions. These revision notes should consist of very concise summaries or outlines of topics covered, lists of essential information, etc. Try and set them out as systematically as you can – may be even by using different coloured paper or pens for each topic.

Some students aim to end up with flashcards showing the minimum amount of information necessary to trigger recall of what they have learned. Remember that our brains work much more effectively when seeking out answers to questions than from passive reading. A suggested revision technique is as follows:

Skim over your notes about a topic, making notes of key points or paragraph headlines as you go; Then read back through thoroughly for about 20 minutes, searching out supporting information for the key points, and making notes of this as you read. Go on to test yourself on what you have read, maybe by making the chapter heading into a question and seeing if you can answer it, using brief notes, diagrams or with a recording. Check out your answer in the test, look for any omissions. Alternatively, test yourself by answering questions from past exam papers. A brief outline answer, as a list of points that could be covered or a suitable diagram, is enough.

Answer one or two questions from each paper fully. This will help you to check out your timing and your style. Look again at these answers after a few days, from an examiner's point of view:

DOI: 10.4324/9781003754244-13

HOW MANY GOOD POINTS HAVE YOU MADE?
HOW MANY HAVE YOU OMITTED?
HAVE YOU ANSWERED THE QUESTION FULLY?
IS YOUR STYLE OKAY?
IS YOUR HANDWRITING LEGIBLE?

Try to be as honest with yourself as you can.

DO NOT MISS CLASSES TOWARDS THE TIME OF EXAMS – YOU MAY MISS OUT ON NEW TEACHING COVERING TOPICS IN THE EXAMS OR ANY REVISION WORK OR HINTS ON WHAT MAY BE COVERED.

DO NOT EMBARK ON LOADS OF NEW READING, THIS WILL JUST CLOG UP YOUR MEMORY AND WILL NOT HELP YOU!

Start formal revision six to eight weeks before exams, but take your individual working pattern and how much you realistically have to do into account.

PRACTICE IN RECALLING THINGS – PRACTICE IN ANSWERING QUESTIONS – PRACTICE IN ASSESSING ANSWERS

Exam Strategies

Plan to finish formal revision a day or two before your first exam and use these last days to:

Tie up loose ends; Check out equipment, etc. you will need for exams; Work through one longer relaxation exercise – over 30 minutes – the calming effect of this can last for two to three days; Avoid any potentially stressful activities during this time, like going to the dentist, long journeys, etc.

Exam Day

Morning Exam

Get up reasonably early and allow yourself plenty of time (no dawn revision, as you will lose freshness and energy). Get everything ready to go well before you plan to leave. Eat some breakfast, or your energy level will flag towards mid-day.

Afternoon Exam

Same leisurely pace. Maybe check over a few notes or things you have found difficult to memorise. Relax for half an hour or so before leaving (listen to music or the radio). Eat a light lunch.

Allow plenty of time for your journey. Plan to arrive ten minutes before the exam starts. Go to the loo! Avoid anyone obviously anxious – it is infectious! Chat to someone, or read the paper, do a crossword or recite times tables backwards! To "warm up" your brain.

Walk in to the exam room as firmly and calmly as you can, remembering to say any affirmation over to yourself that you find useful. (For example, this exam will go really well or I can handle anything that comes up in this exam.) This will help to set your mood. Take a few moments to relax, a few deep breaths, look about you and ground yourself in the room, noticing colours, smells, sounds etc. and arrange your stuff.

The Exam Paper

Read the exam paper through, then read it again, marking possible questions to answer as you go. Then read through the questions you have marked again, very carefully. Note any instructions, compulsory sections, etc. (Highlight these if necessary). Spend a few moments deciding what each question means. When you have decided which questions you will answer, allocate time for each (including outlines), leaving ten minutes at the end.

Most people work on their easiest questions first. This gets you off to a confident start, and may leave extra time for more difficult questions.

Don't start writing out your answer straight away. Spend a few minutes writing brief notes (or a spider diagram, etc.). showing key points you will cover, and possibly how you plan to structure your answer.

Check Once More If Your Plan Is Actually Answering the Question That Has Been Asked

If a question is in several parts, answer each part clearly, with a separate paragraph for each part. Focus on just one question at a time. Get your ideas down on paper in some way as quickly as you can. Don't copy out the questions, and don't spend too much time on introductions to your answers. Try to be interesting. Avoid unnecessary waffle, strings of adjectives, etc. Use words from the questions in your answer – this will link them together. Aim to write two or three paragraphs per page of A4 and vary the lengths of your sentences.

Keep as cool as you can while writing. Keep an eye on the time. If time becomes short, don't panic – take a mini-pause and use a positive affirmation to encourage yourself – a nurturing voice!

Leave a question if it's taking too much time; you can always return to it at the end, even if you have to finish it in note form. It is easier to gain marks from beginning a fresh answer than to try to squeeze additional marks from one you have almost covered. Tell yourself you have ENOUGH time.

If your mind goes blank, just take a few deep breaths, relax a little and try an affirmation such as, 'it will come back to me'. Look around you and ground yourself in the room, and try to ease the tension. Once the pressure is off, missing bits will surface. If you have to, move on, and if you suddenly remember something, note a keyword or two, so that you won't lose the information again and carry on with what you went on to do – go back when you have finished.

Round off answers properly. Don't just stop dead or trail off. Do not worry about what other candidates may be doing; long answers are not necessarily good answers.

At the end, spend ten minutes or so checking through your answers, tidying up if necessary. Check the admin; that the information is correct; and that your answers are correctly numbered.

After the Exam

Avoid post mortems. It is too late to change anything, and you may increase your anxiety about later exams. However, a constructive appraisal of your time management, presentation, etc. could be useful. Do not expect to unwind immediately. Take care if you are driving home.

Aim to Have Some Fun and Lighten Up Before the Next Exam

Case Story of Hassan – Exam Stress

Hassan was referred by the GP for a first full counselling appointment. The referral note indicated that Hassan was very stressed about his third-year final exams, in Computer Science, coming up in a couple of months. He had a history of a long-term fear of exams. He hadn't wanted to take any medication but was open to coming for counselling. He had not experienced any previous counselling or therapy.

Hassan seemed quite nervous, sort of uncomfortable with himself in some way. He was sitting on the edge of his seat and seemed a little bit shaky. I asked him to tell me a bit about his fear of exams and when it had begun.

"Well, I always get very nervous about exams and because my finals are coming up quite soon, I just thought it would be good to seek some help. My house mate kind of persuaded me".

"A lot of students do find exams difficult. There is a lot of pressure around them. How long have you felt like this about exams?"

"I guess probably since about 16, when exams became more important. There is quite a pressure on me at home in India to do well, from my family. It was a big thing for me to come to the UK to study".

"Have you enjoyed the course?"

> "I really have, my house mates have been great and, I've made some good friends, it is just, I guess, I am a bit of a perfectionist, quite hard on myself. It matters so much to my family that I can now get a good job at home. There are lots of good people after every job and I suppose I just want to do well. There is a lot on my shoulders, to be successful".

"How have you found the course?"

"I love computers and the course has been good, but I have never found exams easy. I think I am a more practical person, exams seem like a real pressure to me. That makes me afraid".

"What do you think you are most afraid of".

"Oh, that is easy, it is just not doing well, not getting a good job, letting down my family. It has cost a lot for me to study here and I must do well".

"That does sound like quite a lot of pressure for you". "How have you done in any end of year exams or tests here?"

> "Usually good, but sometimes, I just go blank. This goes back to a kind of fear of performing. I used to hate tests at school. My father is quite strict and expects his children to do well. In particular, I don't want to let him down".

"What have you found has helped you over the years?"

> "Well, I run. I like long distance running. It relaxes me and I find it peaceful. It is lovely countryside around here and I can go off running for an hour or so most days It is my way of switching off".

"Is there anything else that helps?"

"Not really".

"Would it help for you to do some meditation or relaxation exercises. I can give you a couple of hand-outs".

"I think it would. A friend suggested I go to some of her yoga classes on campus, that ends with a meditation".

"That sounds as if it would be very helpful. If you enjoy running, would it help you to listen to a music tape of something that relaxes you as well?"

"I never think to do that, I think it would help".

"Also, just some deep breathing exercises to help you relax, might be helpful".

> "I think I need to give myself more time for things like this as well as revising. I tend to cram in so much reading, that I don't spend time enough to relax my body and then I know the stress builds up. The running helps, but sometimes it produces more pressure".

"What would help you to release that fear, particularly the fear of letting your family down?"

"Well, I know they love me, but the expectations, particularly of my father are sometimes too heavy for me".

"Well, our time is nearly up today, may I suggest some homework for you to do, and that we meet up next week".

"I'd appreciate that".

> "I wonder if it would be helpful for you draw or paint a picture of those expectations, that feel very heavy for you. Maybe you need to see them, feel them, in order to be able to let them go. It is just a suggestion".

"I like that idea, I have an immediate image of them and actually I love drawing, doodling. That actually relaxes me".

"Good, let's make an appointment for next week".

The following week, Hassan came back with three drawings, which were really good. He had obviously enjoyed doing them. I asked him about each of the three drawings.

One was a picture of him with five people on his back, and he was almost stumbling with the weight of them. I asked him about what this meant to him.

"I do feel that, as the oldest son in our family, there is a pressure for me to achieve, perform, help our family to be financially stable. I don't mind that, because I've grown up proud of our family, my parents, brothers and my sister. But, just sometimes it feels like too much responsibility. My father runs his own travel business and I didn't want to work in that. Luckily my two brothers are interested in doing that. I have just always loved computers and I have enjoyed studying Computer Science".

"What would help this picture be lighter?"

"I need time to put down the weight of the responsibility of being the older son?"

"Has that been easier to do, while you are studying?"

"I've had more time to myself, which is quite hard at home. But, the degree itself is a big weight".

Here Hassan shows me the second picture of lots of small shapes spinning and orbiting round and round his head.

> "These small shapes spinning around and inside my head is all the things I am studying, which is not just about computer work, which I enjoy, but having to study in English, which I began learning at around 14 or 15. Languages do not come easy to me. It was an expectation of my father, he wanted me to learn English, so that I could study here".

"Your English is very good Hassan".

"Well, that's the thing, there is a part of me that is a real perfectionist and I've always wanted to do well, but sometimes it just feels like, it is all too much".

> "I can understand that, which is why it is really important that you obviously have things in your life that enable you to relax and 'switch off'. Walking is good. Music is good. Drawing and doodling is a real escape for you".

"I've had the time and space, studying here, to do more of these things, which has helped me. I just don't want to be swamped by 'family' and 'expectations' when I get home".

"What will help you to continue to find space for yourself to relax?"

"Well, this third picture might".

"Hassan held up the third picture, which was him walking away from his family home, having cut a large rope that was coming out from the house and was wrapped around him".

> "I think I need to move out from our family home and find my own space, with friends or even on my own. I've been thinking about that since last week. I still want to see them of course, but not live with them on a permanent basis".

"Would that be a problem for your family?"

"Maybe, I think I need to speak to my mother about it. She is very understanding. I think she would understand and maybe help me negotiate that with my father".

"It might be easier than you think, with the fact of your having been here for three years".

"I hope so. These pictures have really helped me to understand what I need and want and knowing that will maybe help me to fight for them".

Hassan left the room, resolved to do what he needed to do for himself on his return home to India.

In the holidays, I received a card from him and he'd written,

> "I returned home soon after the exams. I want you to know that I got a good, 2.1 degree result. I'm in the process of looking for an apartment in the city, which I will be sharing with two friends – with my family's blessing! (With help from my mum and from you, thank you!)".

I was very pleased for him.

Chapter 12

Neurodiversity Diagnosis – How We Can Help?

"A Steep Rise in Neurodivergent Children Referred to Mental Health Services"

In a recent article written by Louise Eccles, Education and Early Years Editor of the Sunday Times, she maintains that, "The number of children and teenagers referred to mental health services for support with autism, ADHD and related conditions has risen by 28 per cent in a year". She refers to, "The report, by the Children's Commissioner for England, said referrals for neurodevelopmental conditions to Children and Young People's Mental Health Services had gone up from 147,600 in 2022–2023 to 188,700. Children referred for autism face an average wait of seven months, the longest for any condition." She goes on to report that "The annual report found that 8 per cent of all children in England – almost one million patients – now have an active referral to mental health services".

Types of Neurodiversity

The most common types of neurodiversity are autism or autism spectrum conditions, dyslexia, dyscalculia, ADHD – Attention Deficit Hyperactivity Disorder, sometimes called ADD – Attention Deficit Disorder, OCD – Obsessive Compulsive Disorder or Tourette's Syndrome and some other learning differences. While there are some common aspects to neurodivergent symptoms, the individual expression, needs and strengths of each person may be considered to be under this umbrella of neurodivergence but they may each also have many differences. Each individual 'story' needs to be considered as quite unique.

What Helps Clients with a Neurodiversity Diagnosis?

What is most important in the counselling of neurodivergent clients is what they themselves perceive and can tell us themselves, about their needs, their way of seeing the world, about what works for them and what doesn't work for them. The counsellor can offer support by being on the journey of these clients with them, because it can be a lonely place, with their having often been made to feel

DOI: 10.4324/9781003754244-14

'different', 'odd' in some ways and 'lesser than'. In fact, many neurodivergent clients are highly intelligent and because of their often unique ways of seeing the world, they have an enormous amount to offer to our general awareness of the world, relationships and how we function as human beings.

Quite often neurodivergent clients may have found social connections difficult because of being perceived as 'different'. So, building their confidence in the counselling about 'who they are' and acknowledging their many strengths will certainly help them. They have had to manoeuvre in their world for many years and will certainly have learnt many coping mechanisms. As counsellors or therapists, we need to form a strong alliance and level of understanding with all of our clients, but when working with neurodivergent clients, our clients really are the experts on themselves.

One way we can help such clients is for us to become much more familiar with what neurodivergence really is, reading about how neurodivergence can manifest but also reading real-life stories, biographies written about and written by neurodivergent people. If nearly 20% of the world population is thought to have neurodivergent traits, then it is vital for us, as counsellors, to learn much more about these individuals and their perception of the world.

It is widely accepted that neurodivergent people are highly intelligent. Neurodiversity is about the many different ways the human brain processes information. The more diversity there is in this aspect, the wider are our experiences as human beings. Anything that helps us expand our knowledge, our way of thinking, feeling and being is very positive, so we really do need to bring more value to these 'differences' in us as human beings.

Hopefully, in the counselling, there may be a real opportunity for neurodivergent individuals to learn more self-acceptance, more confidence in how to integrate socially, how to manage their power, strengths and differences in the most positive ways, especially in a world that often finds 'difference' of any kind, threatening.

Many neurodivergent students and staff, in particular, have found real support and comfort from walking in a labyrinth. We discovered this on campus from our Labyrinth Experience in 2008.

Our Labyrinth Experience

The University of Kent is fortunate enough to have a beautiful outdoor labyrinth, designed by Jeff Saward, a prominent labyrinth designer and constructed by Hayward Landscapes, specialist labyrinth builders. The labyrinth project here was initiated and primarily financed by Creative Learning Fellow, Dr. Jan Sellers, from winning a National Teaching Fellowship. Her inspiration came from reading about the indoor and outdoor labyrinths at the University of Edinburgh. This led to Jan helping to finance our two labyrinths, in 2008, one an indoor canvas labyrinth and one an extraordinary outside labyrinth, built from 8,000 individually cut York stones which make up the pathway of the labyrinth.

Both labyrinths have been used as tools for teaching and learning; relaxation and reflection; therapeutic support and spiritual development. They are also works of art, particularly the Canterbury Labyrinth, positioned as it is, on a sloping meadow overlooking and carefully lined up with Canterbury Cathedral. I have seen students and staff doing yoga, meditation or simply having lunch enjoying the peace of this place as well as walking, running and dancing in the labyrinth. Children, particularly seem to love it, and I recently enjoyed watching one little boy walk backwards all the way into and out of the labyrinth.

We are very fortunate in Canterbury as there is also a beautiful labyrinth built in the gardens of St. Martin's Priory at Canterbury Christchurch University, a similar one in the gardens of the local Pilgrim's Hospice and a smaller but beautiful one built in a therapeutic centre, just outside Canterbury, in Kingston, called The Quiet View.

A labyrinth group was formed here at the University of Kent with colleagues from the Unit for the Enhancement of Learning and Teaching (UELT), the counselling service, the chaplaincy, Kent Union, the Widening Participation team and one of the college masters. This collaboration was exciting and fruitful, and four of us, two counsellors and two UELT staff, completed labyrinth facilitation training with the organisation, Veriditas, at Chartres Cathedral where there is the most beautiful stone-built labyrinth, which has been well walked since the early 1200s. Veriditas is an organisation at the forefront of promoting the use of labyrinths worldwide. Their website will list any labyrinths worldwide, and there are quite a few on university campuses. The 'miracle' of the Canterbury Labyrinth was that it took only 13 weeks from the initial bid to build it to the opening of the completed labyrinth on the last weekend of the Lambeth Conference, a conference of international bishops and archbishops no less! Anyone working in institutions knows how long it normally takes to get approval through committees. This labyrinth really wanted to be here!

The counselling service promoted many different creative ways of working with the labyrinth including using it as a therapeutic tool for group work and as part of the counselling process itself. Some clients found enormous comfort and peace from regular walks in the labyrinth. It is a wonderful place to meditate, especially for clients struggling with stress, anxiety or panic.

We did find that, in particular, neurodiverse clients really appreciated feeling 'held' by the labyrinth while they felt free to explore both the outside landscape and their own inner landscape. Some of them described the space of the labyrinth as both calming and stimulating; a place where they can 'let go' and safely meet 'whatever is' in those moments. One young male student with a diagnosis of 'autism' was so enthusiastic about walking the labyrinth that he persuaded his mum to come to Canterbury and walk it with him. She was amazed at the difference in him and how much it calmed him.

One way to walk a labyrinth is to focus on the way into the centre of the labyrinth: '**releasing**' something specific that you may feel the need to let go of, which could be stress or worries or just letting go of the outside world generally. At the centre of the labyrinth, it is good to focus on something you may want to '**receive**'. This could be in the form of an answer to a question; having time to listen to 'what is' inside of you; or simply a few moments of peace and relaxation; and '**returning**' as you walk out, may be simply bringing that experience with you, whatever that is. You could also use your time in the centre of the labyrinth to do a breathing meditation.

When you do your first walk on a labyrinth, it can be quite hard to lose that initial self-consciousness. Sometimes strong feelings can come to the surface. People have found themselves imagining walking around the labyrinth with close family members who have died, a very moving experience. Others have let go of negative feelings, traumatic experiences and even repetitive thought patterns. Things can happen in a labyrinth!

Whenever I visit the Canterbury Labyrinth now, there are often children playing and running around them and they just really enjoy the whole experience as 'play'.

There are a number of labyrinths on university campuses all over the world, and some universities have portable canvas labyrinths that can be walked, inside suitably large buildings. You can find a list of labyrinths worldwide and information about them on the worldwide labyrinth locator on the Veriditas Website, contact@veriditas.org.

Case Story of Alice – Obsessive Compulsive Disorder

Alice came for an Assessment, seemed rather anxious, as she took time settling in her seat. She told me she had never been for counselling before, wasn't sure it would help, but was finding it difficult to settle into her course. She was six months into her first year studying maths at university.

She looked tired and tense, looking around the room. She was quiet for a bit and then said, she wasn't sure university was for her. She enjoyed the work but socially was finding it difficult to cope. She told me that new situations had always been difficult for her, and she had been diagnosed as a young teenager with OCD. I asked her how that affected her on a day-to-day level.

She had found school difficult initially but there were two girls she'd made friends with, who had really understood her, both having both been diagnosed with autism, and they just knew what it was like to feel 'different'. She was in regular contact with both of them, which helped, but really missed them not being on campus with her. She had met one young man in her maths group who was also finding it difficult to adjust to being here on campus. He had dyslexia, but they both loved maths and were very good at it. They were quite a bit ahead of the rest of their group.

They had been able to talk about how it felt to grow up feeling 'different'. This has helped her a bit but she hasn't really connected with any of the women in her courses, and she was missing the easy friendships she'd had at home, when she hadn't had to 'explain' anything about herself. Also, she reflected that when she does something new, the OCD gets worse, and it makes her tired, well, exhausted really.

She learnt to drive as soon as she could, the year before coming to university. She'd loved driving and was thrilled to have saved enough money to buy her own car and bring it with her to university. But her discomfort of leaving the familiar environment at home had made her really anxious about driving, and she had begun to have visions of having knocked someone over, so she would stop the car and go back to make sure it hadn't happened. "I know it sounds weird", "but, it feels so real". This was exhausting her and taking away her joy of driving. One of the things she'd loved about learning to drive was that it had made her feel more in control, and now this was happening.

It reminded her of her childhood when she had got really upset thinking she had broken something, even when she hadn't. It was just her fear and imagination, playing tricks on her, part of the OCD. Even though she knew that, it didn't help. I asked her what she had discovered that would make that easier. She thought about it and said, "well, I used to do some relaxation techniques, which did relax me and brought me into the moment and away from my fears".

I asked her what she thought would help now. She replied, "I think I've underestimated how stressful it has been for me leaving school, where everything was familiar, leaving home, where I felt settled and comfortable". "I don't think I took into account how stressful it would be coming to university and having to adjust to everything being different".

I suggested to Alice that she take a walk in the labyrinth, which was built on campus. Alice eventually walked the labyrinth regularly, and it made a real difference to her ability to relax; it just grounded her, and she felt 'contained' by it and so much more in balance in herself. It certainly helped to reduce the frequency and severity of her OCD. She found it useful to focus on 'releasing' her stress on the walk into the centre of the labyrinth, and at the centre, she really felt the peace that she had wanted to 'receive'. She took time out in the centre of the labyrinth to do a breathing meditation. That whole experience had worked for her to relax and feel contained in a way that she normally found difficult.

Alice was a very aware person, especially about the effects of the OCD on her. She decided to come back and have two more sessions of counselling, and she was very effective at thinking up things that might help her. She also made more effort to get to know some of the other students, who may not understand how she thinks and feels, but who might be willing to listen. She really did find the courage to take risks, and it really helped that she had a very good understanding of how she was affected by the OCD. Her acceptance that she could, as she had in the past, find ways around it and work with it, was very impressive. She'd learnt many 'transferable skills' over the years, including how to deal with the OCD, but she had felt stressed by being out of her normal comfort zone and in a very new situation, away from home, at university.

Case Study of David – Autism

David was a first-year student, a month into his course on campus. His parents had suggested he check in with the counselling service on campus. He was diagnosed with autism as a child and has learnt to cope with it reasonably well over the years, doing well at school and he was just beginning a degree in chemistry He came for counselling because it was a big change for him leaving school, although he was going to continue living at home, which was quite close to campus, at least for this first year. He appeared quite anxious, and he sat on the edge of his seat, not really making eye contact.

I asked him how he felt about leaving the familiarity of school and coming to university. "I wanted to study chemistry and wanted to stay living at home for now, until I feel more comfortable on campus", he replied. "That sounds like a good idea, to ease yourself into university life. What else would help you to settle into your course". He thought about it. "Well, I'm gradually getting used to the classes, it was very difficult initially". "I get very anxious, starting something new and on quite a big campus". "On two occasions, I wasn't able to go into the lecture theatre. It's not so bad having seminars and I don't mind the chemistry laboratory, which is familiar to me but the large lecture theatre is a bit overwhelming". "I asked someone if I could borrow their notes and photocopy them, a young woman who lives near me, and is studying here too". "She was at my school, so she knows I find some things difficult".

"Do you have anything that you do that relaxes you, when you get anxious?" "I do walk quite a lot, which, helps me to relax". "At the moment it all feels a bit overwhelming". "Is there anything else that helps you". "Well, I was doing a yoga class, locally, to help me get through my 'A levels', but I'm a bit anxious about going back". "What would help you to overcome that anxiety, it sounds as if it helped you". "Well, it was quite hard for me to come here, for counselling, so maybe I could go back to the yoga class".

> Something else that you might find supportive that we have here on campus, is the labyrinth. There is something very calming about walking in a labyrinth especially for students experiencing autism. It never changes, you walk into the centre and sometimes it helps to focus on releasing anything you want to release and once at the centre, it can help for you to focus on something you want to welcome in, it may be calm, relaxation, balance, whatever you feel you need and as you walk back out of the labyrinth, imagine bringing that with you.

"I haven't seen the labyrinth, where is it? Well, it is directly behind Eliot College and overlooks Canterbury Cathedral". There are a few others in the area. I'll give you this leaflet on it".

"That sounds interesting, I'm willing to go and have a look. I've never walked in a labyrinth. Thank you".

"I hope you enjoy it, it does sound to me that you have been good at looking after yourself, after all beginning at university, with all new people who you haven't met before, is hard for everyone". "You've done well".

David smiled, but still looked very anxious sitting in his chair. "Would it help to do a short breathing meditation here, for say, 10 minutes?" "Yes, I could give it a try". "Okay, find a position that you feel comfortable with in your chair, close your eyes and just take several deep breathes and take as long as you like, breathing in peace, or whatever you are comfortable imagining and imagine breathing out any tension, or discomfort of any kind."

"I'll let you know when the 10 minutes is up". David nodded.

I told him when the ten minutes were up and suggested he take his time slowly to bring his attention back into the room. He seemed really quite relaxed as he opened his eyes. I asked how that had been for him. He smiled, "I didn't think I would be able to relax, but I did".

"What do you find most difficult to deal with?" "Well, quite often I get an upset stomach, but it is that lack of peace, I hardly ever feel comfortable with myself. Sometimes, it makes me angry, sometime sad. I find any change really difficult, so coming here gave me very many sleepless nights and sometimes, it is that overwhelming tiredness that is so hard, that and a constant sort of edginess. I just wish I could be like other people".

"Could you say a bit more about that". "Well, I've been like this all of my life and sometimes it is easier to cope with and sometimes, I just want to hide away. I used to constantly move my hands as a child and people just thought I was weird, but a therapist helped me with that. It can be exhausting to feel, 'different', to have weird thoughts sometime".

What kind of thoughts?" "Oh, sometime I feel like I will never 'catch up' with other people, that I'll never just be 'okay'". "What would 'okay' look like for you?" "I guess I never really feel, still, at peace, comfortable in my own skin. I feel as if I was born 'shaken up' and 'on high alert', almost waiting for something bad to happen. I don't like the bright lights in the big lecture theatre here. It takes me much longer to acclimatise to a new environment. I am better once I get into a routine about everything, which calms me".

"Do you ever feel moments like that?" "Sometimes in the yoga relaxation, lying down, I can feel calm for a while. But, sometimes that makes me sad because as soon as I get out into the world again, I feel myself becoming more and more wound up".

"I'm sorry that it is hard for you. Would it be helpful for you to come along for a few sessions, just for you to have somewhere to talk about it?" "Well, I was really scared about today, but it has been good". "Yes, I'd like to come again".

We made an appointment for the following week. The counselling helped David to settle into university and gradually as he got to know his way around, he made one or two friends in the seminars. He really enjoyed studying chemistry. He even got used to being in the larger lecture theatres. It was not easy for him, but he persevered and made it work for him. David really enjoyed the labyrinth on campus, especially as it combined his love of walking and being outside, and he found it calming. He really 'got it'. David continued with the yoga class, which both energised him and was relaxing for him. He was pleased to have got back to that. After a few sessions, we left it that he could check in for a half appointment, if he felt he needed continuing support.

Chapter 13

Pregnancy, Abortion, Infertility and Miscarriages

Pregnancy and/or Abortion

It can be a real shock for a female student to find herself pregnant at university, if it was unplanned. Sometimes her partner, who may or may not also be a student, will be supportive and want to come for counselling with her; other times, it may be the woman who is left with the decision about seeking an abortion or the decision to go ahead with the birth and make arrangements for herself and her baby after the birth. If she or they decide to keep the baby, then there will need to be decisions about whether the mother and/or the father want to take a break from their work or university or continue with her or their studies and find a nursery place. Many universities have good nurseries on campus.

It may be that both or either of their parents are able to support them, and that is another decision, who to tell and when to tell them. It is often a very hard decision to make for the potential mother, for the potential father and may well depend on the support they can call upon. They need to consider their feelings and thoughts about taking a break from their courses, and or work, if that were necessary. There is a lot to consider in the short and long term, and coming for counselling can really help. There are usually time constraints to consider, practical and emotional considerations. These are decisions which will have consequences for many years to come.

Counselling can be really helpful to allow the mother and father, if the father is involved in the decision, to take some space and time to think through the implications of an abortion and the implications of keeping their child. This is often not an easy decision. However, there is usually good childcare support on most university campuses, which can really help if they decide to go ahead and keep their child.

In the situation of a couple who decide to have a child, while both of them or one of them are studying at university there will also be many decisions for the parents to make in terms of child care, medical support and financial support. Sometimes it is valuable to take the time and space available in a session of counselling to discuss all of the implications of how they want to manage this situation in the best possible way. This may include discussions of whether either the mother or the father needs to take time out from study or get more help with childcare to make this situation more manageable.

DOI: 10.4324/9781003754244-15

Although there are many practical things to be considered, this is all a highly charged emotional experience, becoming parents, maybe for the first time. Counselling provides a real space for you to give all your attention to this new situation, to help you give consideration to your feelings and thoughts about what would most support you to find solutions, insights and help you make the best 'informed' choices and good decisions.

HER CHOICE

Her hands shake
as she pulls out loose threads
from the frayed edge of her denim jacket.
Her hair hangs limp over hunched shoulders.
Black T-shirt covers her expectant body.
Dark shadows invade her eyes.

The seat beside her, conspicuously empty.
She unfolds their options, tastes, digests them.
Each one painstakingly weighed.

She looks out of the window,
pulls back her hair
reveals her youth.
Tension trembles in her
as she struggles to be wiser than she feels.

Her words slow into silence.
Something shifts.
Courage straightens her body.
She takes ownership of their position
and makes her choice.

Miscarriages and Infertility

Miscarriages are relatively common, and most couples go on to successfully have babies. However, it can still be traumatic, especially if it is not the first time. So many expectations and then a disappointment, which sometimes repeat themselves, increasing the natural worry of perhaps not being able to have a baby. It is important to seek medical advice and treatment that would help in future pregnancies. However, it can be very stressful, and many people find it helpful to talk through their feelings and fears by having some counselling.

Infertility can be a real shock and a deep sadness and disappointment for a couple who may have just assumed that they could have children, whether they had thought about it or not before. It may be that there have been no reasons at all for them to think this was a possibility. Of course, the first thing to do is to get medical advice to find out if this is a problem which can be resolved or not. There may well be medical procedures which can help.

If you have got all the advice that you can and this is still a problem, then it would be helpful to look for other solutions, either adoption, working with children in a positive way that enable either or both of you to have contact with little ones. It may be that in your, extended family, you can help out and build relationships with children.

Regardless of how you can mitigate the loss of being unable to have your own child, it can be a real feeling of loss and bereavement, and it is very important to acknowledge this, as well as consider alternative ways of having children in your lives.

It can be helpful to use the space and time of counselling to connect with your feelings of grief and loss about being unable to have your own children. Other feelings which are so important to acknowledge may be the shame, pain, inadequacy and even guilt that the person who is infertile may feel. There may be feelings of anger in either partner of this relationship about the loss of expectations, any feelings of being 'at fault'. What is important is to acknowledge your feelings and to express them in any way that feels most appropriate to you.

Case Story of Jessica and John – Infertility

Jessica is a postgraduate student aged 36, who, more than a year ago, sought out tests for infertility. She was angry and fed up with having been 'messed round with' in different hospitals with a long line of tests and procedures which she was put through and it took so long. She felt it was assumed by her husband, John, that it must be her 'fault'.

Recently, her husband John had agreed, rather reluctantly, to be tested, and it had turned out that he was infertile, which he has been angry about. He has also been unwilling to discuss with her what they decide to do about this now.

Eventually, Jessica decided to come for counselling and asked John to come too; he agreed, somewhat reluctantly, but here they are, and this is the first session.

Jessica describes feeling a sense of loss and failure and 'difference' from other friends and family, who just seem to take for granted that they would have children. She is angry that it has taken quite so long to find this out, partly because John was not very willing to get tested.

John admitted he was reluctant to be tested; he was afraid that it might be his fault, and he had found it difficult to accept. They both seemed quite angry with each other. I asked them how they both felt now about the situation and what they wanted to get out of the counselling.

Jessica spoke first, "I'm still angry with John for not getting tested sooner, he assumed, something must be wrong with me".

John agreed, "I did think it must be Jessica's problem that was stopping us from having a child. I'm sorry now, but I think I was scared that it was my fault. That just made me feel 'less of a man'. It has been very hard for me to accept that I could be infertile. I felt guilty and angry and that I had let Jessica down".

"How do you feel about it now John?"

"I feel bad that I wanted it to be Jessica that was at fault. I am really sorry that I've behaved badly".

"How do you feel Jessica?"

> "I've been angry with John's attitude but now we are here. I just want to put the past behind us and discuss what our options are now. I want us both to stop being angry and be 'real' about what we can do and what we want to do. We have been offered an appointment now by the hospital. I'm prepared to move forward and find out what is possible, if John is".

"I don't want to be angry any more. I feel guilty and bad about being the one 'at fault'. I need to accept that".

John admitted, he'd felt confused, angry, ashamed, guilty, and he thought that Jessica wouldn't want to be with him anymore. They had had a long talk the day before, knowing they were coming here, He'd got very upset. He admitted that he felt a failure being infertile, and he was angry with himself, with her, with the world.

They had begun to really talk about the grief that they both felt. He was willing now to talk about adoption, a sperm donor, to just find out more about what was possible rather than being so focussed on himself as a failure.

Jessica had found out more details of what was possible, of what they could do. She wanted to know if John was committed to doing this together. John felt that his 'male pride' had been really hurt. He was happy to talk to some contacts that Jessic had found, a couple who had been through this whole thing and that by using intrauterine insemination, they had produced two children using donor sperm.

They both felt that at the moment they didn't need further counselling; they had really resolved something within themselves. They both had felt a huge sense of failure but just knowing that there were real possibilities out there of things they could do was really helping them to feel better about themselves. Just talking had built their trust back with each other, and they both said with a smile at the end. "We'll just keep talking!!"

Jessica half-smiled. "I think we both have to forgive each other and face up to 'what is' and 'what we both want'.

John replied, "I guess if you can forgive me, then I do need to forgive myself".

We left it, that if either or both of them wanted to have further sessions, they could contact me via the counselling service.

Chapter 14

Procrastination and Burn Out – Too Little or Too Much

Procrastination – 'Rust Out'

Even though you may be busy with work, you may still feel there is a lack of challenge or excitement in your life. It can be tiring if you are spending a lot of your time doing something you are not energised or excited by. If this is the case and a complete change is not possible for you at the moment, look for ways of spending your leisure time that will challenge or stimulate you. If you create short breaks from work and find something to do that energises you, then you will come back refreshed and more able to work effectively.

Learn something new; that is always a challenge. Notice what happens to your energy around other people, notice which people and what activities lift your energy, and notice who and what leaves you feeling drained of energy. Even clearing a drawer out can lift your mood. If you are experiencing 'rust out' choose to spend your time in a way that stimulates you. You deserve to spend your time in a way that creates happiness and enjoyment. So often we neglect ourselves because we feel that we don't deserve to be happy, and we don't give ourselves that extra little bit of space or time.

Some aspects of your life may be difficult to change right now but think about even one small change that you could make to create some good feelings, which in turn creates a good energy for yourself. Let yourself know if you are bored. You could take a walk, or just go and sit somewhere that creates a change of energy and environment. You could arrange a special event, do something that really stimulates you and gives you a buzz. Think about things you may have done in the past that made you feel energised and that maybe you have stopped doing for yourself. Spend some quality time with people who stimulate you.

Case Story of Tom – Rust Out

Tom's handshake is light and warm. He sits heavily, closed in by his chair, noticing very little of his surroundings. He wears his clothes uncomfortably. His face looks strained. His voice struggles to be heard. He is 48. When he makes eye contact, his eyes look tired with resignation. Tom was working

DOI: 10.4324/9781003754244-16

with computer systems in a company that went into receivership. He was made redundant and decided to use his redundancy pay to come back to university as a mature student and study for an M.A. in computer science, hoping that would give him more job opportunities and perhaps time to think about what he wants to do next. For many years, he has spent most of his time in front of a computer screen, and he has felt trapped inside a cage, the bars of which feel solid, with a kind of powerlessness.

Tom has little interest in doing much outside of his studies especially since his youngest daughter has recently left home to study at an Art College some distance away from home. He had often visited art exhibitions with her, a passion they shared. Tom had had a good relationship with his wife, Carol, but she is getting fed up with him 'numbing out' on an excess of television and occasionally too much alcohol. It is Carol who has urged him to seek help. Since being made redundant several months ago, Tom admits that he has been having occasional difficulties of impotence. He understands that since then he has been feeling impotent in his life. He has not been willing to talk to his wife about this when she has tried to talk about it. He thought coming to university would help his energy levels, which were pretty low. He feels as if he is 'going through the motions', but there is no real enjoyment in the course.

We look at what he **could** do. Tom confided that he has always wanted to go to Art College and as a teenager he had loved being creative, mainly drawing and painting. When his children were young, he used to enjoy painting with them, and his daughter has been so enthusiastic, she has now gone on to study art. We focus on whether he could get back to doing more painting either on his own or by joining an art class in the evenings. He feels that he can't spare the time while he is doing this course, but it is a real struggle for him to have any enthusiasm for this course. His energy feels really low. He is halfway through the M.A. and wants to finish it but not sure what he wants to do with it. So, we have a conversation about what jobs he might be interested in doing and whether he can focus his M.A. dissertation on something that connects with his obvious passion for art. He recognises for himself that he gives up too easily what gives him energy and 'goes along with' the easiest option. This is making him tired. He sees a pattern that he often gives up on himself. He could see a pattern in his family where his older sister was outgoing and successful doing what she loved, which was architecture. He always felt he wasn't as good as her and sort of fell into doing computing at school and then at college. He sometimes feels a bit the same with his wife. They had children quite young but then she went on to study accountancy and has a really good job. It really helps him to see the similarities and how much he has given in and given up on himself.

I suggest some homework for him using artwork. He painted two pictures that represented people, beliefs and habits that block him: a bright painting of his extrovert, successful older sister seen in the painting as much bigger and brighter than him; and a dark fear that he isn't good enough with a barricade in front of him avoiding that colourful life of challenges. The paintings were extremely good, and he really enjoyed spending time doing them. I had also asked him to notice who and what gives him energy and it was obvious that anything to do with painting would be very high on his list. It also helped him to understand and feel for the little boy that he had been and gave him the strength to move on now.

A little further on in the counselling he arrives quite excited. He has thought of a project he could do involving computerised cataloguing in an art gallery in a different way. He has phoned some galleries in London with his idea, and one of them was interested in taking this further for the purposes of his M.A dissertation. He has got advice from his supervisor on the course and together they have devised a possible plan for an interesting piece of work he could do. I had not seen him so animated before.

The fire of enthusiasm that was lit by this project helped him to work and live more effectively. He talked more to his wife about what he was doing here. They sat and wrote a list together of things they used to enjoy doing together that they had both let go of. He wrote a list of activities, places to visit and people in his life that energised him. They took some time out for a weekend away, and what really helped was that they were talking together about this and looking for solutions together. When we finished the counselling, Tom brought me a small, very beautiful and colourful painting which he had done, which has pride of place in my counselling room.

Increasing Motivation

Thinking Process: Messages, Beliefs and Decisions

Our strength and confidence can get stuck by messages like: I have to be a winner; I must be really busy; I must be more than anyone else; I must be caring for others above myself; I must be perfect; I must be polite; I must be angry and loud… otherwise I'm not wanted. I will be rejected; No one will hear, see, notice me; No one will value me; I'm not good enough; No-one will love me….

Recognising these messages, noting how much you use them to stop yourself from moving forward with ease in your life is a good beginning to changing them. We can turn them around by using positive affirmations instead.

Our power and motivation can get stuck by messages like: I can't paint; express myself; speak up; speak out; sing; dance; sculpt; write; play; garden; sew; be disciplined; take charge of my life; take the lead; change job; risk adventure; play a musical instrument;….if I do, I will be ridiculed; be bored; ashamed; get it wrong; not be as good as….; get attacked or bullied; be rejected; be insecure; be unsafe;

feel vulnerable; fail; it would upset other people; I'd be scared. I can't do it... just for fun; ...because I want to; ...because I like it; ...because it makes me feel good.

Notice yourself using 'I can't and change it to either 'I can' or 'I don't want to right now but I can'. It increases our self-confidence, security and feeling safe in the world, which can enable us to enjoy moving forward in the world.

Taking action, risking changing something, is fundamental to improving our enjoyment and ease of movement in the world. To feel the fear, acknowledge our vulnerability and do it anyway. Act and you will move, one small step at a time.

Our potency and ability to rise can get stuck by messages like: I don't deserve to have... rest; ...play; ...freedom; ...say no; ...good relationships; ...good health; ...a successful life; ...choices; ...a happy life; ...abundance; ...enough; ...what I want; ...love.

Letting go of guilt or social conditioning can enable us to achieve abundance and fulfilment in our lives:

Recognising that our lives are being lived now and that we are basically here to find happiness, joy, fulfilment, love, will help us to be motivated to live our lives the way we want to ***now.***

Can you think of up to six messages or beliefs that you could say to yourself that would enable and support you to move forward in the world positively and productively?

It would help us to move forward by becoming aware of our choices, how we choose and what we choose. Small choices at first and then it will become easier to risk making larger choices.

Think about what has worked for you to motivate you to take positive risks and move forward?

What Else Increases Our Motivation to Change?

VALUES – Is whatever you want to be motivated to do important enough? (If it is, you might need to clear space, emotionally or even practically, by getting rid of any lack of self-belief, by getting rid of excess paperwork, clutter, work and meetings that you don't absolutely need).

ENERGY – Is what you are doing giving you enough energy?

SETTING REALISTIC EXPECTATIONS (Self-Esteem is Success over expectations)

KNOWLEDGE; INFORMATION; SKILLS; TRAINING (You may need these to help with your motivation)

BELIEVE YOU DESERVE THIS.

Making Friends with Feelings

Those old messages, beliefs and decisions that we've made, go on to influence our feelings, which then guide our patterns of behaviour. We need to notice and normalise our feelings in a way that is positive and constructive; After all we can choose to encourage ourselves with feelings that will help us.

ANGER – NEEDS TO BE RELEASED OR EXPRESSED: Exercise, any physical activity; Talking them over with someone; Creative expression.

SADNESS – NEEDS COMFORT: Expression of your feelings; Comforting food; Comforting music; A hug; Relax with a good book;

FEAR – NEEDS PROTECTION: Visiting places where you feel safe; Consider how you can keep yourself safe from worry or harm; Get more reassurance; Ask for support; Take care of yourself. Avoid stress and negativity.

SHAME, GUILT, SELF DOUBT – NEEDS TO BE TIME LIMITED: Forgive yourself easily; Let go of self-doubts; Build inner confidence; Distract yourself; Build self-confidence; Be positive towards yourself.

JEALOUSY AND ENVY – NEEDS TO BE PUT INTO PERSPECTIVE: Distract yourself; Find alternative satisfaction or gratification; Take good care of yourself and your needs.

POST-TRAUMATIC STRESS: If you have experienced a seriously traumatic event in your life, it would help you to seek help for this so you can 'debrief'. Go for walks, rest in beautiful places, anything that you find relaxing.

JOY, WHAT MAKES YOU HAPPY AND FULFILLED: Find interests that give you joy. Knowing what you enjoy helps you move in the right direction, for you. Spend time out in nature. Spend time with people who make you laugh. Spend time doing what gives you pleasure. Create a good balance in your life.

NOTICE AND AVOID SITUATIONS, ACTIVITIES AND PEOPLE THAT HAVE A NEGATIVE INFLUENCE ON YOU AND STOP YOUR MOTIVATION OR CREATIVITY

Negative Attachments and Patterns of Behaviour

Attachments to things, messages, beliefs, security, rebellious responses, adapted responses, perceived safety. Attachment to people and places that can cause us to act out, be stuck in ingrained habits or patterns of behaviour. **We can choose to let go of these.**

Become aware of your choices, how you choose, what you choose. Know you can let these go: small choices at first, then it will become easier to let go of the old and entrenched choices that lead to our negative behaviours. **We can choose to let go of these.**

How we let go: We need to become conscious and aware of old patterns, habits, choices and attachments. We need to take full responsibility for new decisions to make the change, do the work, create the will that increases our motivation to take the risk to change, one step at a time.

Positive Behaviour

As human beings, our need for change is often pitted against our resistance to change. We get used to responding in a certain way, it might be adapted behaviour, (being good) or rebellious behaviour, (anti-authority). Familiar patterns of behaviour can then become ingrained. We can choose to recognise old patterns, habits or feeling stuck and let go of any unwanted entrenched behaviours.

Take full responsibility for your new decision to make the change, do the work, create the will that will increase your motivation and just do it, one step at a time. It feels good!

Our relationship with ourself is fundamental to improving our enjoyment of who we are, which can motivate us to enjoy the present moment and make the most of now.

Think about one thing that you would like to change. Part of living, loving and letting go, wanting to be the best we can be. What frees us from early messages which have become beliefs, or decisions, have maybe created feelings which cause attachments, which have become habitual patterns of behaviour, too heavy to carry around.

Too Much – 'Burn Out'

Many of the people I saw for counselling with 'Burn Out' have stopped listening to their bodies or their tiredness and find it difficult to conceive that they can take time out. 'Burn Out' is accumulative over a long period of time and can be caused by 'driving' ourselves too hard, often fuelled by self-criticism. It can be difficult to stop. A bit like having been on a 'treadmill' for so long, you forget how to make it stop, and it feels really odd to 'step off' and feel the ground again. That is exactly what is needed to become 'grounded' again. To get back the balance, take the time out you deserve, to have fun, play, do something quite unrelated to work, often the greatest need is to do absolutely nothing. This does not mean that the work will not be done. Someone with 'Burn Out' is rarely working effectively or achieving as much as they could be. Ideas, life, work, relationships and creativity become stale with 'Burn Out', and it is possible to reach a place where you literally have nothing left to give. As to how much time you need to take out from work, that will vary according to how out of balance you have been. What is important is that you take enough to get back your enthusiasm, creativity, ideas and energy. It is vital that you re-think how you can balance your life with time out to play, to relax in a way that gives you energy rather than just activities that lead to you 'numbing out'. Many people, recognising that their energy is low, seek to replenish their energy through a variety of drugs: alcohol, nicotine, caffeine, sugar and others. Although you might feel energised in the short term, in the long term if you are having too much of any of these, they will deplete your energy further. You may need to take time out for exercise or time to 'recharge your batteries' and do absolutely nothing.

Case Story of Jenny – 'Burn Out'

Jenny bustled in, slightly late, gasping for breath, took off layers, set down bags and books she was carrying.

She unreeled her story at speed, watching the clock as she had another appointment straight afterwards. She filled the room and chair. I felt as if we were, 'speed counselling'. Jenny recounted a list of things: "I've been off sick with colds, flu and recently pneumonia. I've put on several stones of weight in the past few years, have pains and heaviness in my arms. The doctors, here on campus, referred me for counselling. I have two children of 9 and 10, work part-time and study part-time. I call in to see my parents several times a week, both are rather frail. My husband, Neil, works abroad, sometimes for weeks at a time. I'm often 'on call' for my 5 younger siblings when they have difficulties".

Jenny bought so many other people into the room with her that it took a while before she ran out of steam and stopped talking. I asked her what she imagined that her body was wanting to say to her. For the first time, she was fully in the room, quiet, thoughtful, tears welled up as she whispered, "I want to get off this treadmill". She cried and was desperately wiping her face and nose, afraid to make a mess. Jenny was aware that she got her value from caring for others, admitted that it was hugely difficult for her to ask for help. She imagined a mountain of people standing on her shoulders as she stood holding the hands of her children. Overweight seemed an appropriate manifestation. Her support network was limited to her husband, often working away from home and one good friend and neighbour, often in crisis herself. Occasionally, her sisters would be supportive, but it was most often the other way around as she was the oldest sister.

Jenny resisted the idea of taking time out for herself until we focussed on how unavailable she would be to her family and friends if she continued to be unwell, as she was, and became even more chronically ill. She began to realise in the counselling how difficult it was for her to focus on herself. Her life was full up with other people. She thought about how she could shift the balance and eventually risked asking her neighbour to have her children for a whole day, so that she could spend a day **on her own** in London. She had loved trips to London as a child. She treated herself to a tour in an open-top bus, had a luxurious lunch and attended the matinee of a play she'd really wanted to see. She risked asking her siblings to take more responsibility for their parents and even to babysit for her when she wanted to go out to the cinema with a new friend from her course. She was far from the top of her list but now she was at least on her list!

In the next session, she told me that she had talked to her husband on the phone about the counselling and they had agreed to talk, when he got back from this trip away, about him working less time abroad. He did realise that there was too much responsibility left with Jenny, especially as she was studying now. He was genuinely apologetic and was willing to see if there was anything he could do.

Jenny was an extraordinarily bright woman who gave enormous time, effort and care to other people. It seemed that she now realised, just how much responsibility she was carrying for work, home, studying, and family. Jenny said, quietly, "I've always got my value as a person, from a young age, by caring for others. It has always been hugely difficult for me to ask other people for help". "I realise now, no-one else can change this for me. I have to do this for myself".

When we ended the counselling, after four weeks, she had been up to London for another day out. Her husband had got agreement with his company to increase his working hours, back in the UK. Jenny's sisters were more available to have time with her children, which they and the children were enjoying. Jenny just felt less stressed and, most important of all, she was much more able to realise when she needed space and had got used to asking for more time for herself. Not surprisingly, Jenny's health was gradually improving.

Tom and Jenny both knew they were 'under doing' and 'over doing' but in reaching out for support, insight and empowerment from an outside source they were moving themselves to a higher level of willingness to take responsibility for making the changes they needed to make.

Finding a Healthy Balance

All types of stress, or being out of balance, if ignored for long enough and allowed to become chronic, can lead to a variety of physical and psychological symptoms and indeed most 'dis-ease' results from chronic stress or being out of balance and literally a lack of 'ease' in your life. Becoming ill is often the only time many people are willing to take time out and re-assess their lives and lifestyles. It is important to recognise when you are beginning to experience stress so that you can manage it before it creates a serious health problem. Once recognised it is possible to reduce your levels of stress by re-balancing the various aspects of your life, although it will need a commitment from you to do so.

Time out for all of us, needs to be built into our busy schedules on an hourly, daily, weekly, monthly and annual basis in order to achieve balance and good health in our lives. A good balance of work, rest and play. This really does help us to work more effectively.

Any swing into 'Rust Out' or 'Burn Out' can deplete our energy and create ill health, lack of interest in life, a desire to 'numb out on life' or over stimulate ourselves on: people, alcohol, food, adrenaline, a variety of drugs, cigarettes, television, sugar, coffee and other addictive substances and behaviours.

A healthy balance is good for our general health, our feelings, our mental health, our energy levels, our sleeping patterns, our relationships with ourselves and with others. We make better decisions in every area of our lives, when we give priority to finding a healthy balance, on a daily basis.

Chapter 15

Relationships – Together, Turning Water Into Wine

Relationship with Ourselves

Our number one relationship is with ourselves. This is the most important relationship you will ever have; you might as well enjoy it, but certainly it is good to learn to honour it!

What I learnt early on in my work as a counsellor is that life can be a journey towards freedom, and many of our relationships increase the awareness, sometimes the pain and sometimes the joy, of being on this journey. Relationships and our capacity to care and love are vital to us. The most important relationship for us to work at is our relationship, understanding, acceptance and awareness of ourselves.

We all know that if we are feeling good about ourselves, things and other people that can annoy us, frustrate us, sadden us aren't nearly so all-consuming. We are not so attached to reacting negatively to other people if we feel good about ourselves.

Counselling works to help people grow and change. It can be a catalyst to change, helped by the neutral relationship of trust between client and counsellor. It is effective for us to find a safe, well-defined space with someone, who we don't know at all and use this space to hear ourselves speak about our own life. This especially encourages an increased awareness of the relationship we have with ourself.

If we can take the power to change even one thing in our lives, it is a transferable skill to change anything else we choose. We all get stuck and make mistakes, but we can also all learn from the mistakes that we make. Part of counselling is normalising this process. There is great relief to know how similar we all are. It is just what it is to be human!

So Many Different Relationships to Learn From

We have so many different relationships that are important to us: love relationships, friends, family, pets and sometimes, a relationship to something, which seems so much larger than we can ever be, alone. It is very important in our relationships to recognise who and what in our lives increases our energy and who and what

DOI: 10.4324/9781003754244-17

decreases our energy, and how we choose what we do about this? We have other relationships that are important to us: our relationship to friends, partners, family, work, to studying, to nature, to cars and driving, to money, to countries, to pursuits...the list is perhaps endless. We have passions that drive us to do particular things, and the loss of them can be enormous. I remember working with a client who was no longer able to play football, which was his absolute passion, and there was enormous grief for him to deal with at this loss in his life.

Working mainly on a university campus, it was interesting to notice what happens in the relationship to academic work and how even that can stem from patterns of relationships within our family. I used to find that sometimes, if students had difficulties with their academic work, it may have links to their relationship with male figures in their lives, and sometimes, if they had difficulties with emotions, it could stem from their relationship with women figures in their lives and other variations on this.

Sometimes, as a counsellor, we can feel like a detective helping our clients to look for those patterns from childhood or later life that can cause 'blocks', 'attachments', 'conditioning', 'habits', 'learned limitations', unrealistic expectations and can even cause them to give up a part of themselves. Deepest of all are those survival strategies that we take on as children as a necessity 'to survive', that can work for us temporarily but can prevent us from growing into our fullest potential as adults, if we become too attached to them.

When I first began relationship counselling, I remember reading that marriage/live-in partnerships are a space where both love and hate can be contained, and any other feelings you can imagine. Living with another person accelerates the process of learning considerably. In all of our relationships, it is the easiest thing in the world to blame or want to change the other person. However, it is not possible to change anyone else. Everyone is a gift to us as they present lessons for us as to how to change ourselves. I've found I have often attracted just the right person into my life, long and short term to teach me the lessons that I needed to learn. Some people give us energy, and some people take our energy. But relationships help us to learn and become more aware of ourselves.

If we can take the time and intention to change even one thing, we can gain the confidence from the fact that we are capable of changing. We **all** get stuck, and we **all** learn by making mistakes. Part of counselling, for me, that was most rewarding was **normalising** this process. There is great relief to know how similar we all are. It is just what it is to be human! I found, especially in young adults, there is such a fear that there is something **wrong** with us and as soon as that notion is released, there is such a relief and everything gets a little bit easier. Quite often, I have worked with a client who repeatedly says negative things about themselves and really may not have noticed. It can be a challenge to ask them to just **notice** how many times they make the same negative comment about themselves. Often it has surprised them and even enabled them to be able to see the humour in it, which can help them work towards stopping it!

There are certainly some things that help a relationship work: humour, giving ourselves and our partners space, curiosity, an open mind, a willingness to become more aware, more trusting, more accepting, more forgiving and more playful. These help us normalise how we are and how we relate, free of **expectations** and **seeking perfection** – two things that can cause much heartache in a relationship, especially with ourselves.

The harshness of how children can be treated and the capacity we have as human beings for joy and love, despite difficult beginnings in life is amazing. That extraordinary human spirit that we are all capable of is one of the true wonders of the world!

Counselling works to help people grow and change by creating a special but also well-defined and safe relationship of trust between client and counsellor. It has to be confidential to have the level of trust that is required. It is especially helpful for us, as clients, to hear ourselves speak out about our own lives. This encourages an increased awareness of the relationship we have with ourselves, when we can really hear ourselves. As a counsellor, we are listening carefully not just to what is said, but also to what is not said.

Emily Rupert, an American Transactional Analyst Psychotherapist, ran workshops about less healthy ways of merging in relationships: 'YOU ARE ME' or 'YOUR OR ME' where we may look for people who are either 'like us' or there is a 'power struggle' where only one person can be 'right'. She regarded a healthy way of relating as 'YOU AND ME', where we can accept differences and relate without feeling threatened or diminished by each other, a position where both parties are valued and empowered by the relationship, by themselves and the other.

Some relationships are a joy in our lives and give us energy; some relationships may take our energy; some relationships may indeed present us with a lesson to learn about, when we need to walk away from a truly harmful relation. After working for some time in a 'Women's Refuge', I was humbled by the courage it had taken for the women there to walk away, often from very damaging relationships. But, there are many less extreme examples, of people who can cause us to feel tired, even exhausted in our relationships. We may need to find a way to limit the time we spend with them and sometimes that may also mean walking away altogether.

A good quote from Charlotte Joko Beck's Book, 'Everyday Zen', Harper/Collin, 3 March 1997:

> ...There is no way that is superior about relationships in helping us see where we're stuck and what we're holding on to. As long as our buttons are pushed, we have a great chance to learn and grow. So, a relationship is a great gift, not because it makes us happy – it often doesn't – but because any intimate relationship, if we view it as practice, is the clearest mirror we can find.

What I have learnt from counselling, my own therapy, meditation practice and from being married for many years is that the freer we are: of 'past luggage' and 'attachments', the more we are able to be creative, loving, playful and compassionate. This then enables us to live in the moment more, be productive in our own lives, and have happier, freer relationships. Possibly the most important thing that grows out of this freedom is the capacity for us to laugh at our shared humanness, those small things, that we can make so important when we are feeling grumpy, tired, on edge, overworked etc.

'Coming Out'

For many students, leaving home and arriving on a university campus can make it easier to begin to live their lives more honestly. Especially for students who identify as LGBTQ, defined here as Lesbian, Gay, Bisexual, Transgender or Transsexual and Queer. Often coming to university offers an opportunity to begin to be more comfortable with their 'real self'. University life has always tended to be a 'Rite of Passage', and this can be true for students sexually. University or College can be a place where there is simply more acceptance of an LGBTQ identity. More freedom from oppression, less bullying, which some people might have experienced in their growing up. It is also an opportunity for many such students to have access to counselling to enable their process of 'coming out' as their true selves, getting support for who they really feel they are. There is still a lot of misunderstanding, fear and prejudice against LGBTQ people. An interesting YouTube Channel recording that might be of interest is 'Philosophy Tube' by Abigail Thorn, it has 800,000 followers, and she expresses some of her feelings of what it is to be Transgender in a very authentic and compassionate way.

Beginning at university can be a good time to get counselling support to help you begin to live your life more authentically. It can help students to begin or to continue with their process of 'coming out' in whatever way is most honest and true for them.

Sexually Speaking

Sexual issues can be a reflection of what is going on emotionally. For those clients who are inhibited or inexperienced, it might be useful to have a whole session on helping the client to become more comfortable talking about sex. Also, it may be helpful to have a discussion in supervision if and when it might be appropriate to refer any client on to a sex therapist for further help.

Bullying from Yourself or Others

One way that some people find useful to notice when they are being bullied, by themselves, is to 'Name that Voice'. Notice the negative voice and imagine it taken out of your head and placed on your right shoulder, whispering negative messages in your ear. You could even draw it, give it a name or character, like a cartoon character, no longer frightening and maybe slightly ridiculous. The idea is to distance it from you, a safe way to treat a bully. Then what you most need is to imagine a positive voice which you could visualise sitting on your left shoulder, to counteract the negative voice. You could give this positive voice a name, a much-loved relative who did give you support, love and encouragement, a fictional or an imaginary character who you think might also do the same. Most important of all is to imagine this person being completely on your side whispering encouraging and supportive comments to you. This can work if you are feeling bullied by someone else. If you experience someone in 'bullying mode', imagine them as a cartoon character who can do you no harm, to make them less powerful to you in that moment. Take time to breathe more easily, you do not have to take on and take in what that person is saying or the anger and aggression that they are using to say it to you. This is something coming from the 'small child bully' inside them, actually it has nothing to do with you. Let go of this feeling and let go of being a 'victim'.

A Short Meditation for You

Meditation: Shut your eyes, make yourself as comfortable as you can. Take a few slow, deep breaths and allow yourself to be present in this moment, leaving the busyness of life outside the door. As you sit here for a few moments, think about something that you really like about yourself. Imagine feeling acceptance for the person you are right now, as being the best you can be in this moment. You're the only person who lives with you for the whole of your life from birth to death. Can you honour that for a few moments by breathing in gratitude for your body, your mind, your heart, your whole unique self as you are in this moment. Push away any criticism, judgements and instead focus on unconditional love for yourself, as you are now. Imagine feeling full up enough with that love until you can maybe smile even just a little, with yourself. Sit with this feeling for a few moments and then, when you are ready come back into yourself, feel yourself being the best that you can be right now.

Drama Triangle

There is a lot of energy in joining in a communication that is part of the drama triangle. It is indeed 'dramatic'. We can all find ourselves, sometimes, taking on the role of: 'Rescuer', 'Victim' or 'Persecutor'. They are interchangeable roles, and the one thing that links them is the energy involved in this communication. It can take your energy and be exhausting to stay in any of these roles. Notice if that is what happens to you in any of your relationships or communications. Assertiveness is the path out of each one of these disempowering roles. Yes, even the Rescuer can be disempowering of others. Remember the other side of Helping is Control!

Case Story of Marjorie and Bill – Relationship Counselling

Marjorie is a postgraduate student and had talked to a nurse in the medical centre about difficulties in her marriage, while discussing the results of a blood test for anaemia. The nurse had suggested that she and her husband, Bill, seek some counselling together. She had asked Bill to come as well, and he had agreed. Marjorie began talking, saying that she felt tired all the time, but although some of that was the anaemia, she was really unhappy in their marriage.

I asked what she wanted to say to Bill about this. She turned towards Bill and, with tears in her eyes, she said, "I thought you would know what I need" "I didn't expect you to be so silent with me and really quite rude sometimes". "I feel as if I'm the one trying to make it alright for you and the children, even though I'm hurting". "I've felt ashamed that I'm always feeling tired". "I know now that is partly to do with the anaemia, but life feels like all work and no play".

I asked Bill what he felt about what Marjorie was saying. He was very quiet but said, "I'm sorry Marjorie, I do get angry, I'm not sure what you want from me". "I feel as if I'm programmed, ready for action, I suppose I've always felt someone wants something from me, it all feels like a pressure".

I asked Bill if he knew where that feeling came from. He thought about it and said, "At work I feel I can't fail, can't let the side down". "Sometimes, when I get home, I feel as if I have no energy left". "I think it goes back to having been the oldest child at home too. I felt that I had to be the 'man' in the family, when my dad wasn't around, especially when he was working away from home, even when I was quite young". "I don't remember playing as a child. I think my anger is about wanting to push people away, because sometimes it feels as if everyone wants a part of me and sometimes, I just have nothing more to give".

"That's how I feel too Bill, I feel hurt and I do feel you push me away". "I feel a bit overwhelmed sometimes, doing this degree, but it is something I want to do for myself, it's important to me and it will lead to a better job eventually".

"I know Marjorie and I'm glad you're doing it for yourself and for us". "I'm really sorry I haven't talked to you about any of this". "It's' been hard when you just don't talk to me. I think I've always felt a bit like no-one hears me. It was a bit like that as I grew up. I've always been a hard worker but haven't always taken time out for myself. It was hard for me to sign up for this M.A., to do something for me. I realise that I feel guilty about taking this time for myself and that makes it hard for me to ask for more help from you Bill, but I do need your help, if I am going to be able to finish this M.A. successfully, it is a lot of work for me".

"I want to support you Marjorie, we both agreed that you do this course. My anger really isn't with you Marjorie, I think it goes back a long way. I know I had to grow up fast and often there was no-one around me who I could ask for help. I had to sort things out on my own".

Both Marjorie and Bill have been holding back a lot of how they were feeling, neither of them really able to put themselves first in their own families. Once they began to talk to each other and say the things they had been keeping to themselves. It just felt like a relief and a release for both of them.

We went on to talk about where each of them could get more support. Bill needed more support at work, and Marjorie wanted to have more time to connect with the friends she was making here. They were rarely able to get out together as a couple and had not been very good at asking for other family members to babysit for them. It was feeling a bit as if it was all work and no play.

The following week they came back with a plan for getting more help from other family members to babysit. Neither of them was used to asking for help. So, coming here and asking for help in the counselling was a good beginning for them in taking care of themselves individually and as a couple.

When they came into the next session, they looked so much more relaxed, they smiled, they laughed, and now they had truly given themselves permission to ask for what they wanted, from each other, from their family and from friends, who were willing to give a helping hand, so they got more space and time together as a couple.

Chapter 16

Self-Esteem

I'm Okay, You're Okay

What Is Self-Esteem?

Self-esteem is how much we value ourselves. As we arrive in adulthood, our level of self-esteem reflects how nurturing and supportive the people around us were. The way our parents, teachers, family and friends have regarded, judged, loved, respected and behaved towards us influences how well we regard, judge, love, value, respect or behave towards ourselves. None of these people existed in a vacuum, so their behaviour towards us will have been influenced by their own experiences, beliefs, cultural, religious, political and social norms. So, we receive messages about ourselves from **many** different people for **many** different reasons but they are opinions in that moment, not facts. It doesn't mean they are true. Such messages are not set in stone!

We may not have had control of how other people viewed and treated us but we can take control of our future view and treatment of ourselves. We can choose to get to know our strengths, skills and positive aspects and we can choose to build on these and learn to love, approve of, accept, value and care for ourselves the best we can.

If we are fortunate, we will have received a balance of positive and negative messages, but for many of us, self-esteem takes a pounding during the process of childhood, especially given the pressures that exist in schools, family life and in Society as a whole. There is much emphasis placed on 'performance'. There is pressure to achieve at younger and younger ages: goals and grades; assessments and inspections. Children have become highly measured commodities. The fear, uncertainty, self-doubt and negativity which can be generated by such a system can be a breeding ground for low self-esteem. Some of us have learnt to exaggerate our mistakes and excel at self-doubt and self-criticism. Some of us grow up having to deal with the stress and trauma of poverty, loss and separation, abuse, ill health, even the effects of famine or war. This can damage our confidence, our ability to have faith and trust in ourselves and the world around us. Luckily, we can turn this around and build positive self-esteem.

It is a freedom for us to emphasise what we **are** achieving, what we **are** capable of, what we **are** doing well and **how loveable and amazing we are**. Challenges,

DOI: 10.4324/9781003754244-18

change, mistakes and crises are a part of each of our lives, and it is from such experiences that we learn our best coping strategies and become aware of our many human strengths and abilities. We need appreciation for this, especially from ourselves. It helps us to build confidence if we acknowledge our strengths and positive skills, **at the very least to ourselves!**

Building High Self-Esteem

One of the major tasks for us as maturing adults is to become wise, and it is wise for us to build the best possible relationship with ourselves. Some of us have high self-esteem in some areas of our lives and maybe not in others. To feel good about ourselves leads us to be powerful in our lives and can help us to transform outdated negative beliefs and behaviours into positive beliefs and behaviours. As we increase our self-esteem and our confidence to do things better, it builds on itself! If you nurture and feed a plant, it grows strong and healthy and produces the best flowers and fruit. We are the same; we become much more able to develop talents and gifts to take out into the world – **if we enable ourselves to blossom!**

The first step of regaining self-esteem is to notice how we talk to ourself. Sometimes I have worked with clients in counselling, and I notice that they have used the word 'stupid' about themselves several times in the first ten minutes of the counselling. Often people are really surprised about this when it is pointed out to them. I've noticed too the number of times we may say, 'I can't'. This can be disempowering and is often untrue, especially if it is a judgement of ourselves too soon. It helps us to become aware of how we speak to and about ourselves.

The most important relationship in our life, the longest lasting and most intimate, is our relationship with ourself. We are constantly talking to ourself. It helps us to notice how we **speak to ourself**, how we **speak about ourself** to other people, how we treat ourself, how we feel about ourself. Notice how we could be more positive and kind. We all need love, support and encouragement. We need to become our own best friend. When this relationship is good, other relationships, **our life in general, runs more smoothly!** We need to emphasise our strengths, the things we do well and what we like about ourselves. We need to promote ourselves to ourselves and to the world in the same way that we would a friend.

Building a Solid Centre

One way we build a solid centre inside ourself is to imagine a tall, solid tower running through the centre of our bodies from our feet to the top of our head, made of bricks. **Every time we do something positive for ourselves**: reward ourselves for something we've done well; buy ourselves a treat; visit somewhere we've always wanted to visit; phone a friend who encourages us; do something that gives us joy – listen to lovely music, read something that inspires us, buy a single flower or a postcard to enjoy, take time to walk somewhere relaxing and peaceful, visit an art exhibition which inspires us, make ourselves a lovely meal. Imagine that this adds a solid brick to that tall internal tower, strengthening us at our very centre. Then, imagine that each time we do something that harms us: put ourself down; put up with something or someone that annoys or harms us; smoke; eat or drink too much so that we feel bad; hoard too many things around us so that our space is uncomfortable. Each negative action takes a brick out of that centre and weakens the strength and power of that brick tower which can make us feel more vulnerable and weaker in our very centre. So, if we can think of more positive things to do, the more commitment we make to ourself, the better we will feel. **We are worth it!**

Affirmations

It can be helpful for us to use affirmations. If we think of a positive statement about ourselves or something we've done well and just say it over and over again to ourself as we are walking along, as we are waiting in a queue. If we do this and notice what happens in our body, we can feel a lightness of step, a lift of energy. Just as when we smile or laugh it has a real 'feel good' effect. By using positive statements, we can re-programme new messages into our self-awareness and consciousness, which can build our self-esteem.

It can be helpful to give a few minutes to think about what we are grateful for about ourself. Gratitude about our many gifts, good health and well-being is a vital part of moving forward positively. We could buy a special card, with a picture that we identify with in some way and write in it a list of things we enjoy about ourself and keep adding to it. How much better it would be to fall asleep thinking of positive things we have done that day. Often, **we can be good at dwelling on any negatives** but the positive things might make **you fall asleep with a smile on your face!**

You may like to choose one of the following positive statements to say to yourself a few dozen times. You could breathe it in slowly as you are sitting in a relaxed place or just before you go to sleep. Notice your energy levels change and keep going, even if it sounds awkward at first.

Positive Statements to Begin With, Until You Can Create Your Own!

I can handle anything that comes my way.
I trust myself.
Life is sweet and so am I.
I welcome risks that expand me/my life.
All is well inside and outside of me.
I know this (meeting/seminar/presentation/interview) will go well today.
I belong in the world as an equal.
I am loving myself more each day.
I recognise my own successes.
I am alive to joy, play and laughter.
I am powerful and I love it.

It can take effort and work to regain a realistic and positive perception of ourself. If we allow ourself to know and recognise what we are good at and realise our potential in different aspects of our lives, then we may begin to recognise what a gift we are to the world and then we may take up our proper space.

Case Story of Grace – Self-Esteem

Grace is a third-year law student, whom I see for an initial half-hour assessment.

She seems very aware and has already identified that she can be very negative towards herself and feels that she never quite lives up to her image of how she 'ought' to be. She admits that she sets herself high standards and is a bit of a perfectionist towards herself. She tells me that even when things go well, she minimises her achievements. She realises herself that she is much more encouraging of other people and if they get something wrong, she finds something good to say, but she doesn't do this for herself.

I ask her how she would feel if she gave herself the same kind of encouragement that she gives other people, especially if she gets something wrong. Grace smiled, "I guess I would feel that I don't deserve it. I know I'm hard on myself". I ask her where she thinks this idea of herself being undeserving comes from.

"She sits very still in her chair and her eyes filled with tears. She tightens her hold onto her chair and seems to suddenly take up less space in her chair, in the room".

"I'm sorry to be upset".

"You really don't need to apologise for having feelings here Grace".

Grace smiled through her tears. She was quiet for a bit and then took a deep breath.

> My mum and dad are very hard working, dad is a scientist, mum is a busy G.P. My brother is getting ready to join the G.P. practice and has done really well. They are all high achievers. I've always done okay, but I have always felt that I don't quite measure up, especially to my older brother. He is quite a hard act to follow.

"Are you enjoying your course?"

> Yes, I really enjoy it, I'm doing okay and hope to get my law degree. I'm looking for a place in a small law firm that works with refugees, I want to do something that matters to me. It won't pay as much as a bigger, more corporate law firm, but it's what I want to do. My parents are a bit disappointed.

"It sounds as if you've really thought about what you want to do".

"I have. I know I want to make a difference. I am hard on myself. My parents have always had high expectations of both of us".

"It sounds to me Grace, that you know what you want to do and that's really good isn't it"

"I suppose so".

"Are you aware of how you talk to yourself, think about yourself".

> I guess it's been quite hard holding my own in our family. Being the youngest. I think my brother, Ashley, always got or even, took, more attention. He could be a bit of a bully sometimes. I did feel he was quite cruel when we were younger. He would break my toys or hide some of my things sometimes.

"Do you think he felt the pressure on him sometimes".

"I've not thought of that before, maybe he felt there were higher expectations for him, as the oldest. In some ways, I don't think there were as many expectations on me, being the youngest".

"Have you ever talked to him about it?"

"I haven't, we're not very close. Maybe I will, I can see I've made assumptions. I've kept myself to myself, when maybe he might even have been an ally".

We make an appointment for the following week. I suggest that it might be helpful for her during the week to just notice how she speaks to herself, how she thinks about herself, to notice how she feels about herself, whether she is judging herself a bit harshly sometimes.

Grace came back the following week for a full first session of counselling. She sat in her chair, more relaxed than the previous week. I asked her how she wanted to use today's session. She smiled,

> I've really noticed how I speak to myself and I'm not very nice to myself. I really heard myself being hard on myself. I realise that I tend to talk to myself the way my mum does sometimes. She is probably the person who is hardest on me, really only when she's busy, and she often says, it's because she knows I can do better. Actually, it kind of made me smile because I realised, after last week, I don't have to do that. I don't think I really noticed before.

"That was great that you really listened to yourself and that you know you have a choice".

We both laughed.

> I realised too how judgemental I am about myself, even over small things, my bedroom being untidy, my writing being too small, my essays, I read

> through them so many times, they don't have to be perfect. Then I noticed that I'm not very good at asking for help, for a lift with friends, to borrow something. I feel I need to be self-sufficient. So, a couple of times I did ask for someone to take a book back for me to the library and I asked someone to get something in town for me. I don't do that.

"And did anyone object?"

"No" and she laughed. "They really didn't mind at all".

Grace paused and had a big smile of her face and then said:

> Then, I decided to ask my brother to meet me in town for lunch at the weekend. He was very surprised. We hardly ever do that. Anyway, I told him I was coming here and what we'd talked about. He was astounded, but he opened up to me that he also felt bad some times that he wasn't good enough. He also felt the pressure to 'do better', 'get it right'. It was bizarre that we have never really talked to each other about anything 'personal'.

"So, you deciding to get help, has been helpful for your relationship with your brother too?"

"It was really weird. I felt we were kind of 'making friends' for the first time. We don't talk about ourselves much at all, either of us".

"How did that feel for you?"

"It felt so different, it felt good. I still can't quite believe it. I think he enjoyed it too".

"That was very brave of you and I hope you can build something together that helps both of you".

"I think we both want to do it again".

"Well done, Grace".

At the end of the session, Grace decided that she had broken through something important for herself, so she decided that she didn't feel she needed another appointment for now. She was very pleased with what she had achieved, with friends, with her brother and most of all with herself.

Case Story of Cheryl – Sexual Self-Esteem

Cheryl had been for an assessment a few weeks earlier with another counsellor, and this was her first full counselling session. In the assessor's notes, it seems that Cheryl was having a problem with feeling able to have a sexual relationship with anyone, caused by low self-esteem, which was rooted in an abusive sexual relationship she had experienced with a long-term boyfriend in her hometown. She was studying English and was halfway through her first year.

In the Assessment, there had been a discussion about how much she hated her body. After some discussion between the assessor and Cheryl, she agreed to seek out a foot massage with a woman practitioner, as a way of doing something restorative for her body. This sounded like a good idea. Cheryl wasn't sure she would be able to do this but was prepared to think about it.

I saw Cherryl for our first session. She had a quiet voice and seemed quite shy. I asked how she had felt since her assessment. She told me, "I did go for a reflexology foot massage". I said, "Well done, was that difficult for you to do?"

She answered, "It was hard for me to do, but the woman who did the massage was nice. I think it really helped me, just to have something good for my body".

"What would you like to talk about in the counselling today", I asked, wanting her to feel that she had the choice here.

"I wasn't sure at first, when I made the appointment, but the assessment was helpful. I do realise how much this relationship I had with my ex-boyfriend at home has damaged my feelings about myself and my body".

"I'm really sorry that you have experienced that".

"Thank you", she replied. "I know I need to talk about it, try and understand how that relationship has affected me, maybe find a way to let go of the past".

"Did it help you to talk about it in the assessment".

"It did, it bought up some very painful feelings, but I understand that talking about it is a good way of being able to let it go".

"What would help you today?"

> "I think what I want to achieve long term, is to feel good about my body again. It was really helpful to have a foot massage, just something that felt positive for my body. I've booked another appointment, so that's good".

"Well done, Cheryl, I'm so glad that was helpful for you". She smiled.

"What would you like from today".

> "I think I need to just stop punishing myself. I stayed too long in a relationship that was horrible. I don't know why. I almost felt mesmerised, that I didn't deserve better. I feel angry with myself for continuing to see him. I don't understand why I did that. I think I hate myself for not just walking away".

"What do you think stopped you from doing that".

Cheryl really thought about it and was quiet for some time.

> "Some part of me felt I deserved it. Some part of me was scared of what he would do to me if I did walk away. Also, I was afraid of losing my

best friend, June, who was his sister. She didn't know how bad it was. I was almost one of her family, we'd been friends from junior school. The whole family used to talk as if we would end up being married. I was close to everyone in the family except the closeness with him was a lie".

"That sounds as if it was awful for you. Was there anyone you could tell?"

"Not really, my dad was away from home working on oil pipelines, my mum worked full time, my older sister was married and lived about 30 miles away. They all thought that June's family was looking out for me. They lived over the road and I'd always known them. They did all look out for me, until they didn't, in fairness, I'm not sure they knew what he was like. I was afraid of him, he pretended to be kind, he would buy me things and it was like he controlled me and I didn't know how to break away".

"How did you manage to get away to study here at university?"

"I began to see it as my way out. I was pretty good at school, particularly good at English".

"He would try and sabotage my work and distract me, but I found a way to study in the library at school and I told a friend, who lived on the other side of town and she let me go to her house in the holidays sometimes. She was a good student as well. We studied together. I couldn't have escaped without her".

"You did so well to find a way out of being there".

"It wasn't easy, he was secretly violent and really hurt me. Since being here at uni. I've got good advice from one of the women G.P.'s. It was her that suggested I come here".

"Well, I think you've done amazingly well to plan your escape, get to university and now wanting to heal the past. Do you still see this man?"

"Never, I don't often go home and luckily he is working away from our town now, permanently, in fact I think he is living with someone, poor woman".

"Well done. What do you need to do to reclaim the part of you that was so badly hurt?"

"I'm afraid of getting into any other relationship. I'm afraid I wouldn't be able to look after myself if I get involved with anyone. I just don't know how to trust myself again".

"I have a suggestion, that maybe as a first step in reclaiming your relationship with yourself, maybe you could write a letter to yourself, to say whatever you need to hear yourself say to yourself or what you need to do for yourself. Next session if you want to read that out to yourself here, in an empty chair, and have me as a witness, I'd be happy to do that. It feels important for you to make the decision about exactly what you need to get the trust back with yourself".

"Yes, I get that". We made an appointment for the following week.

In this second session, Cheryl looked quite tense, but she had had her hair cut really nicely, and she had taken care about what she was wearing.

"I've written a letter and I feel ready to read it out to myself".

We put another chair out for her to talk to, which had a cushion in it that represented herself. She took out the letter and was ready to read it out.

She read it out in such a strong voice, and I could see how much Cheryl has grown and is now capable of protecting herself from anything.

Dear Cheryl,

I want to read this out to you and say how glad I am that you've got away from **him,** but now I need to reclaim all of you. I was very young when I got into this abusive relationship and I didn't know how to help you. I didn't want to tell anyone because I felt stupid for not protecting you. So, first of all, I now forgive you, I didn't know people hurt each other like that. I didn't feel protected at home because dad was away so much and mum was working. Jean had her own family and was just too busy to help me. I didn't want anyone else to know.

I know I did well to get here to university, despite all the abuse and pain. I made it out. I found a friend who helped. But, I got myself out and I'm proud of that. Now I want to let **him** go, from every single part of you. I want him gone, for good. I hate him but I want to let that go too, so it doesn't eat you up. I never have to see him now because he lives far away and doesn't come back to see his family.

I know coming to university has helped you to let go of him and make a life for yourself. Now I need to get my body back for myself. I've been scared to go out with any other man and I know that if I really let **him** go, you will be free. I know what to look for in a relationship and it isn't **control.** I've learnt a lot. If anything goes wrong again, I have learnt how to get help and where.

I love you lots, I'm proud of you.

Cheryl

Cheryl felt so strong and had come through so much. I felt very proud of her, too.

We left it that, if she needed another session for any reason at any time, she could come back. She didn't come back.

I watched Cheryl walk down the corridor; she walked with real confidence and balance.

Chapter 17

Stress, Fear, Pressure and Panic – It Takes My Breath Away

Remember, What We Focus on, Tends to Grow!

There are usually some areas in our lives where we do feel as if we have control to make changes. This may range from major changes such as changing jobs or changing country, to finding a way of doing the things we are asked to do, in our own way. We need to recognise and choose areas of our lives where it is possible and appropriate to fight for change and encourage ourselves to do this with courage and in a way that is assertive and effective. Pressure is often connected with a lack of self-expression as well as feeling out of control. Feelings that are unacknowledged, unrecognised and unexpressed can create a negative energy as they build up inside of us, a bit like a dam. If we are angry, it may not be useful to tell the person concerned but we can go away and write down our feelings, even write them a letter that we don't send or express our anger in other ways. I once worked with a female client who would buy up old crockery at Jumble Sales and keep bits and pieces in her shed, and when she got really angry, she would go down to her shed and smash it. It hurt no one and gave her a wonderful outlet for her feelings. If we are afraid, it is useful to look at ways we may need to protect ourselves and talk kindly and calmly to ourselves about how we can actually keep ourselves safe. We can also reassure ourselves that to be afraid is totally normal and is part of our being human. Fear can turn into panic when we feel we should avoid it at all costs. We can then become afraid of being afraid. Normalise it, and it becomes manageable. If we are sad or sorrowful it is helpful to give space to allowing ourselves to go fully into those feelings at an appropriate time and give a dignity to our sadness; in this way, those feelings do not crash into the rest of our lives and stop us from working effectively.

If we are frustrated by having limited ways of expressing ourselves in our working life then it is vital to look outside for ways of expressing ourselves creatively, physically, emotionally or in some other appropriate way. It is important that we are able to feel there are areas of our life over which we do have control.

Stress

A certain level of stress is essential for a healthy and creative life. Healthy stress helps us to work at our optimum levels of intelligence, creativity, power, energy

DOI: 10.4324/9781003754244-19

and willingness to risk. Challenges, change and crises need to be normalised and happen to everyone from time to time and we often deal with such things extraordinarily well, learning new coping skills, compassion and increased awareness of our many strengths and abilities. Some people thrive on high levels of stress, which for others could be draining and traumatising. In my work as a counsellor, I have been humbled and amazed by the extraordinary capacities that clients have demonstrated to find solutions to the tragic, traumatic and painful events in their lives both as adults and as small children.

One way to reduce stress can be for us to identify any 'negative voice' or 'whisper' that comes from ourselves in a self-punishing, self-judgemental way. We can all develop a pushy, critical parent figure. If you have ever experienced this, imagine it sitting on one of your shoulders, even draw a picture of it or think up a name for it. Think about how long it might have been there. Get to know this negative inner voice as this makes it easier to deal with. Don't be persuaded by this 'inner tyrant' to fight back with 'an inner rebel', who might insist on you doing nothing or wasting time in response!

Instead, imagine an encouraging, nurturing parent figure sitting on the other shoulder, who makes encouraging comments to you and tells you how well you are doing. This is a voice which allows you to recover quickly from any stressful situation, not dwelling on it. This is a voice that helps you to talk to yourself in an encouraging and kind way. You could help this positive self-talk by thinking of a list of five positive things you have done during the day, just before you go to sleep – try this every night for a week and then you could just do it occasionally when you need to.

Stress only becomes problematic when there is too much, for too long, or when we find ourselves feeling out of balance or being overwhelmed by negative blocks and limitations. If stress is allowed to accumulate, unacknowledged and ignored, it can become embedded in us as a 'normal way of living'. Then, it can create problems for us. It is this problematic stress that I refer to from now on.

In recent years, schools and universities have endured many changes, sometimes reduced financial resources, which may have meant a reduction in the staff/student ratio. Also, there has been the worldwide covid pandemic, which created very specific difficulties for students and staff. Such challenges have also brought opportunities to introduce new ways of working and communicating.

Beginning university is a lot about managing change. Counselling has a role to play in helping students manage to navigate an effective path through the demands, stresses and conflicts involved in such changes. Counselling can provide feedback, positive intervention and preventative strategies to support students cope with change and illuminate the strengths and inner resources that will enable and empower them to prosper.

When we are counselling students, we need to understand the whole person, their self-perceptions, their past, their relationships with people around them and their experiences within their educational experiences so far. If ignored, it can develop into increased feelings of **stress, fear**, **pressure** or even **panic attacks.**

Fear

Feel the Fear and Do It Anyway – According to Susan Jeffers "Act with confidence and grow into it, one step at a time". "If you knew you could handle anything that came your way, what would you possibly have to fear".

"Five Truths about Fear:

1 The fear will never go away as long as it continues to grow
2 The only way to get rid of the fear of doing something is to go out…and do it.
3 The only way to feel better about myself is to go out…and do it.
4 Not only am I going to experience fear whenever I'm on unfamiliar territory, but so is everyone else.
5 Pushing through fear is less frightening than living with the underlying fear that comes from a feeling of helplessness". (Jeffers, 1987, p.30)

When new students arrive on campus, it's all new, so it is a good opportunity to take a risk. When it comes to choosing companions and friends, we need to notice who and what gives or takes our energy. If we feel drained, we probably are being drained! Don't be afraid to find new people to be friends with, who give you energy.

We all need to set ourselves realistic expectations. When we exercise muscles, if we move them 70%, they improve and become more efficient. 70% is a great goal to aim for, because perfection often doesn't really exist, and may not be the best expectation for us; it can be exhausting!

We need to think about what's worked for us in the past to motivate us. What's encouraged us to make a change or achieve a goal? Believe that we deserve to do well. Believe that we can do well. Remember that it's very human that our need for change is pitted against our resistance to change. We get used to responding in a certain familiar way, which can be **adapted** (being 'good') or which can be **rebellious** (anti-authority). Familiar patterns of behaviour can become too **comfortable**, then **habits**, then **attachments** (much harder to change then). Sometimes we need to change them, to see what happens, to see if it helps or hinders us. A student on a university campus is here to learn, to get advice, to grow and mature.

Case Story of Peter – Fear

Peter was suffering from quite bad acne, had low self-confidence and little self-esteem. He had the most beautiful dark blue eyes hiding under long, dark eye lashes but he looked uncomfortable with himself; he found it hard to make eye contact, looking down a lot, and his hands were shaky. He was wearing a jumper which looked too tight. Although he was 19, he looked closer to 14 or 15. His tutor had suggested that he might benefit from some counselling as he seemed quite nervous and jumpy when he did any presentations, and he was finding it harder and harder to communicate what he knew.

Peter had arrived early for his counselling appointment. He came in to the counselling room and looked quite uncomfortable in himself. He sat down and shifted anxiously in his seat. He looked rather pale, had a slight twitch in his right eye. His hands were shaky. He looked as if he wanted to run from the room. I asked him to tell me a little about himself and why he had come for counselling. He is studying maths and is in his first year. He had grown up not too far away but wanted to stay on campus. He was close to his mum, who had suggested to him that he might benefit from having some counselling. He felt a bit distant from his father who Peter described as a quiet man who was a research chemist in a pharmaceutical company. Peter had a successful younger brother, Mark, who was outgoing, good at sports and had just been accepted into medical school for the following year. They shared a love of computer games and got on pretty well.

Peter told me he had grown up feeling rather nervous and shaky, and he felt a bit embarrassed about this, especially when he was in the lecture theatre or in seminars. It was all just a bit new and he was finding it hard to make friends. He felt quite shy around new people, uneasy. I asked what he felt uneasy about. "I don't always know what to say, I'm afraid of getting things wrong". "I suppose I never felt I measured up to my brother Mark, who comes over as very confident". "My dad is quieter but it doesn't stop him doing things. I've always held back a bit, I think I'm afraid of what people might think". I asked him what may have made him feel like that.

Peter screwed up his eyes and the twitch in his right eye got worse. He looked pale and scared. He had tears in his eyes and he took a deep breath. "Well, I was bullied at school by a boy in the class above me". "He would wait until no-one else was around and he'd punch me on my upper arm, really hard". I said to him, "that sounds horrible". He cried and wiped his nose. "It was horrible" "I was really scared, and he would threaten me that I would be for it, if I told anyone about it". "He knocked me off my bike once, luckily onto the pavement rather than into the road". "I've never told anyone about it".

"He sounds like a real bully". "He was". I asked Peter, "How long since this last happened to you". "Well, it must be nearly two years ago because, thank goodness, he and his family moved away". "But whenever I'm at home I look for him everywhere". "I'm still so scared of meeting him. I was even worried he could have come here to university. I always feel I'm looking over my shoulder". "That's really unpleasant for you Peter".

"What do you think you need now to feel safer, in yourself, wherever you go". "Well, this may sound silly, but I even thought of doing, self-defence lessons". "It doesn't sound at all silly, if it is something that would help you feel that you could defend yourself, then it seems a really good idea". "What about finding out if there are any classes on campus".

For the first time I saw Peter smile, and he had some colour in his cheeks. "This sounds really important to you Peter". "I think it is". "I felt so helpless". "Have you told any of your family or friends about this bullying?" "Honestly, no, I felt so ashamed that I couldn't cope with it". "I just didn't know what to do".

"Well, you may find that they really want to help". "I'm willing to talk to them". "I guess, I felt so helpless, I was terrified about coming to university, in case I met him or someone else like him here".

I asked Peter to sit and take some deep breaths in and out, very slowly, for just over ten minutes. He did and then he smiled. "Wow, I haven't felt like this for a long time". "I can feel my whole body relax in a way I can hardly even remember".

Peter came back for one more session, three weeks on. He had actually signed up for a series of self-defence classes and met another student there who introduced him to a beginner's boxing class held in the local town. Amazingly, he was enjoying the physical exercise, as well as learning how to protect himself. Also, he had opened up to his family about what had been going on, and they were very supportive, especially his younger brother, who shared that he'd been bullied in the top year of his junior school and had been scared to say anything to anyone. This in turn, led to a conversation at home with their dad and with their mum about why they had both felt unable to say anything to them or to each other. It seemed to have been a good learning lesson all round about how important it was to be able to be vulnerable.

Pressure – Taking the Lid Off

Pressure is about feeling out of control of our life, and people have described feeling that their body or head will burst or explode. There can be a build-up of frustration or negative energy often caused by the 'bottling up' of feelings or unexpressed thoughts and a sense of being overwhelmed. A sense of being prodded, pushed or pulled along faster than we can comfortably manage, which is disempowering and can leave us feeling quite inadequate. Words battened down can sink into a deeper form of pressure.

So how can we get control back again? It can be enormously helpful to prioritise the work that we have to do and to divide it into manageable portions. Focussing on what we can do now rather than piling it all up together and using it to weigh us down and slow us down. There needs to be a recognition and acceptance of what we cannot change right now. Resentment about something that is not within our power to change at this moment can waste a lot of energy and cause much unnecessary frustration. Of course, we need to express our feelings and talk over situations and relationships that are causing us concern but do consider our time and energy as a valuable commodity. We can get stuck in our thoughts about someone or something we cannot control. It is difficult sometimes but it may be helpful to focus instead on something we do have control over.

Panic

Panic attacks can be a symptom of different types of stress. All types of stress, if ignored for long enough and allowed to become chronic, can lead to a variety of physical and psychological symptoms and indeed much 'dis-ease' results from chronic stress or distress and literally a lack of 'ease' in your life. Becoming ill can often be the only time some people are willing to take time out and re-assess their lives and lifestyles.

It is important to recognise when we are beginning to experience a low level of panic, which could then turn into panic attacks, so that we can manage it before it creates a serious health problem. Once recognised it is possible to reduce our levels of panic although it will need a commitment from us to do so. If panic is allowed to continue to become more extreme and debilitating, it may lead to regular panic attacks, which can be very distressing. This situation would then certainly benefit from counselling or drug treatment and may even require longer-term therapy from a doctor or a psychiatrist.

Case Story of Jacqueline – Panic

Jacqueline was early for her first appointment and immediately got up from her seat in the waiting room to greet me. Her bubbly energy and warm smile accompanied her into the counselling room. She had lovely shoulder-length auburn hair and was dressed in smart navy trousers and a royal blue shirt, which accentuated the blueness of her eyes. I noticed that despite her easy smile, she held an expression of someone who had been startled, and although she sat back in her seat, there was a sense that she may jump up at any moment and head for the door.

Jacqueline was studying for a psychology degree, now that her two daughters were more self-sufficient, at 12 and 15. She is in her first year and is doing well. However, she had decided that she needed help with a problem which she had only ever shared with her husband.

In her teenage years, she had experienced occasional panic attacks, which she had learnt to manage and hide from most people around her. They had lessened in her mid-twenties, when she'd had her children partly, because she became adept at avoiding situations that triggered them. However, since beginning her psychology degree, they had increased so that she feared that the other students and staff would begin to notice.

Jacqueline had been devastated as a teenager when they'd begun. She could go out with friends for a drink and be fine and then another evening, she would suddenly experience symptoms of intense terror and find that her throat closed up so that she physically could not eat. Her hands and legs would shake uncontrollably, she experienced palpitations, her feet and hands became very cold and she was always terrified that she may faint or pass out. She learnt to control, slow and deepen her breathing, which seemed to help. It happened most, when she was eating in a restaurant. So, she would sometimes avoid holding any food on her fork, pretend to eat, which meant pushing food around her plate to look as if she was eating something. She discovered a myriad of excuses to avoid eating out as much as she could and generally, she became an expert at hiding this from other people.

She did go and see her doctor, who prescribed tranquillisers, which made her feel drowsy and disconnected so that she rarely took them. She was afraid of any chemical side effects and of becoming dependent on drugs. These panic attacks had become slightly worse towards the end of her first year, especially as she became busy doing a project and revising for end-of-year exams. At their worst, she was convinced that she was going mad. She knew there was a counselling service but, she'd been used to managing on her own and frankly felt embarrassed at the idea of telling anyone about this. Somehow, it felt more difficult because she was doing a psychology degree. However, in the vacation, she talked it over with her husband, and she decided that she would seek help when she got back to university. It had taken a lot of courage for her to come for counselling.

I asked what the main triggers had been for her. Mainly, it seemed to be triggered by eating out in public, usually in a restaurant. But, it could also be triggered by any public performance, talk or presentation, perhaps because she felt more vulnerable then anyway. She became adept at hiding it and appearing confident and calm. However, her body would become so tense that she had some extremely painful headaches that would often cause feelings of nausea. She was terrified of being sick, had been all her life. She had gradually developed a fear of the fear itself, which was her constant companion.

Over the past two years, her panic feelings had become more intense, partly because she was less able to avoid situations which were triggers for it. It was difficult for her to avoid social events both in support of her husband's career and because of her life as a student, often eating in public places and refectories on campus. This made her feel more vulnerable again.

I asked Jacqueline to tell me more about herself, including what 'messages' she had about 'how she began in the world'. Jacquline was a younger sister, and her birth had been somewhat traumatic because the umbilical cord had been tight around her neck, so there had been some panic and fears for her life during her birth, according to her mother. She had been planned and wanted by her parents, who had always wanted two daughters as companions for each other. Her older sister bullied her at times but on the whole Jacqueline held her own. Her mother was kind and loving if rather over protective and maybe tried to 'hang on' to Jacqueline, as the youngest child. She felt close to her father, and he would encourage her to be adventurous, but he was often busy working.

I asked her about family meal times since eating was an issue. Her father had been a bit strict about manners at the table and 'eating everything on your plate'. But, on the whole, meal times were times of conversation and family time. Recently, in the summer she had asked her older sister about food and meal times when they were younger, and her sister had told her, for the first time, that when Jacqueline had been about five or six, she had started choking, eating out at a restaurant on holiday in Devon. Jacqueline had been very upset and her mother and sister had both been scared. Jacqueline's father had patted her hard on her back until she coughed up a bit of food. Jacqueline had no recollection of this at all, but it may have been a factor in her fears of eating in restaurants and her issues around food.

So, it seems as if there were two traumatic events to do with food and choking in Jacqueline's early life: her birth experience and the choking incident. Also, she felt her mother had always been somewhat overprotective of her. She had put this down to being the youngest child.

She was aware of feeling an inner conflict between her desire to 'risk' and move out into the world, a confidence reinforced by her father, and a feeling of being unsafe maybe a shyness to 'speak out' and be herself, which was also prevalent in her mother.

Jacqueline found it particularly helpful to do some relaxation exercises and breathing exercises to use when she felt any feelings of panic rising. It also helped her to know where it might have come from. She found it helpful to imagine being able to free herself from any sense of 'being trapped' in a social situation. She decided to practice feeling free to excuse herself from any room at any time, so that if she needed to do this to escape a 'panic reaction' she could. She practiced, excusing herself from the counselling room and going outside for a few minutes. This empowered her to use this as a healthy escape mechanism, from any sense of being trapped in a social situation, if she needed it in future.

One of the hardest things for Jacqueline had been to tell people, choosing wisely who she could trust, about her feelings of panic. She had spent so long hiding her vulnerability and pretending that she was always in control that this was difficult for her. However, it freed her to be more herself and brought positive responses from other people who wanted to support and help her. It had helped her to come for counselling and feeling free enough to ask for help!

Jacqueline came back for a short assessment a few months later as a 'check in'. The panic attacks had become far less frequent and much less debilitating. She felt she could understand them and handle them. If she had any such feelings, she remembered why she felt like that, and she knew the feeling would pass. She also found it helpful to have regular aromatherapy massages and Cranial Sacral Therapy treatments, which continued to help her release the deep tensions she had been holding onto in her body.

Self-Care

Think how similar fear and excitement are; sometimes they can get confused. Notice how other people feel just the same about new experiences. Our feelings are a common part of us that link us to every other human being worldwide. Feelings are a natural part of our healthy process of coping and survival, and they can be very uncomfortable. It is helpful to be able to say something positive to ourselves, **'I can do this'**. **'I can cope with this.'** **'I'm doing okay'. 'I'll feel better soon'. 'People who get most scared are usually intelligent and sensitive'**. The way we speak to ourselves is our best support. We can use our creative imagination positively for ourselves rather than against ourselves. We always have a choice to see a glass or ourselves 'half full' or 'half empty'. We can choose to emphasise what we do well, being okay, believing in ourselves, focussing on what we get right! The most important relationship we ever have is with ourselves; we can choose to be our own best friend! Buy yourself some treats, it can be a postcard, some music, a single flower, a magazine, something that makes you smile.

We all gather unhelpful behaviour patterns; outdated survival strategies; negative self-talk; old and outdated messages about ourselves or other people; limiting habits, beliefs and conditioning that can become ingrained attachments. It's part of growing up and explaining the world and ourselves to ourselves. Fortunately, with maturity, wisdom and self-awareness about which of these help us and which of these harm us, we can decide to change them, let them go. This old luggage can be heavy, too heavy. Choose what you are willing to change and just do it. Begin with one small change, and it becomes easier to achieve the larger things. It's a bit like a room that we've been using and not clearing things away, we need to find a place for everything, and some things need throwing away! Doesn't it feel good when you have a good clear out! Come to think of it, take some time to tidy out a drawer, your bag, a file – order can bring us calm, peace, satisfaction and a good feeling.

Use Your Breath

Breathing meditation or breathing exercises can really help reduce stress, fear, pressure or panic attacks. It really helps to take a few deep breaths, before we begin something stressful: an exam, a talk or presentation. Just breath in and out evenly and deeply, it helps us to relax, be present to ourselves and focus on what we are doing. If you are doing it at home, you can close your eyes, breathe deeply and picture a special place that is safe and relaxing for you. It may be a place that is familiar to you or from your imagination. If you use it often then it becomes a safe place to go. It can be useful to imagine breathing in something you need: courage, peace, confidence, patience, calm or joy. It can be useful to imagine breathing out something you want to let go of: fear, doubt, disappointment, frustration, sadness, panic or tension. Ground yourself wherever you are, take in everything, the colours, temperature, shapes, smells, sounds, feel your body relaxing in this place and return to it any time you are stressed, afraid, feeling pressurised, feel a sense of panic or need some inner support. Also, have plenty of exercise, walks, swimming, dancing, going to the gym, whatever gives you the most pleasure.

Chapter 18

Suicide and Suicidal Thoughts

Suicide Risk Assessment

Always check out any references a client makes to wanting to hurt or kill themselves. Don't be afraid to ask your client directly. This is more likely to lower any anxiety they may have, knowing you are comfortable to talk about this, will indicate that you are more likely to be willing to intervene and help them.

Assessment

Assess past suicidal behaviour:

- Is there a history of past suicide attempts? If so, how serious were these?
- What is the client's assessment of the seriousness of any previous attempts?
- How does the client feel about the outcome of any previous attempts?
- Had they been alone, or was there someone around at the time?
- What was the outcome of past suicide attempts – did the client seek intervention, were they rescued accidentally, were they hospitalised?
- If there is no history of actual previous attempts, ask if the client has ever felt suicidal before. If yes, ask what helped them to recover.
- Have there been any suicide attempts or actual suicide in their family? If so, who was it? When was it? and What is the client's relationship to them?

Assess current suicidal ideation:

- Has the client made a plan to commit suicide? How serious is that plan? Is it specific or more abstract thinking about a plan?
- What would be their preferred method, means and availability of their intentions?
- Do they want to live or to die?
- Do they intend to act on their plan?
- What reasons do they have for living?
- Do their suicidal thoughts feel frightening to them?
- Do they welcome these thoughts or want them to go away?

DOI: 10.4324/9781003754244-20

- Do they have specific thoughts about the specifics around their death, the funeral etc.?
- Do they think about it fleetingly or is it a persistent preoccupation? (daily, weekly, all the time?)
- If it is persistent, how do they manage these suicidal thoughts?

Assess current situation:

- At what point is it in the academic year? (academic work deadlines, examination time etc.)
- Is the client experiencing particular work or financial pressures?
- Does the client have a helpful social support network? (Are they living alone? In a shared house? Do they have sufficient family contact?).
- Has the client experienced any recent trauma or particular stress? (The death of a friend or family member? The ending of a relationship? Coming out as a gay person? An academic failure?)
- What is the level of their depression? (good to check out their sleeping patterns, general health, general mood, level of tiredness, eating habits, etc.)
- Are they experiencing any drug or alcohol abuse?

Interventions

- Be reassured that the very fact of this client talking to you about this is an indication that they want to be helped and supported.
- Communicate your concern and let them know you are glad they are seeking help.
- Encourage your client to talk about their reasons for wanting to kill themselves and what might have triggered this in them, and feed back to them that you really are hearing them: For example, "It sounds as if you are feeling: rather hopeless, lonely, sad, a bit of failure, lost, depressed right now". Ask them if they would be willing to share with you why they are feeling that way.
- Show your understanding that they may believe that suicide is a solution to their problems, but it is a **permanent** solution to a, very likely, temporary problem. Agree to explore with them other options.
- It can be very helpful to make a 'no harm contract' with your client.
- However, if you have any serious concerns that there is an immediate risk of suicide, find a colleague to consult with and support you. (If there is no one else around, do contact your supervisor or other colleagues whom you can ask to help you.)
- Review with your supervisor or colleague the possible need for hospitalisation of the client. If that seems necessary there are two avenues to follow: Either **voluntary** admission, you could then ask the client for the name of a contact who would be willing to transport them to hospital, if no one is available you could tell the client, you would like to contact an ambulance or medical services

for 'immediate transport' for them. Or **involuntary** admission, you could then tell the client you are contacting emergency or other medical services to arrange an Emergency Consult, or to arrange 'immediate transport' and then phone one of the emergency numbers, either on campus, or in the immediate community.

- If hospitalisation is not indicated, but you still have serious concerns, set up a follow up appointment for the client to see you within the next few days, if possible, and share your concerns with your supervisor or a senior colleague. This may need to be followed up by making contact with the nearest medical services, usually on campus. Make sure your client has a contact phone number for the medical services, including sick bay, on campus. It may also be helpful to give them the number for the Samaritans locally.
- Even if you have no immediate concerns for the client's safety, it would be good for you to tell the client that it is normal practice to contact the client's doctor if we have concerns that a client is at risk, as mentioned in our confidentiality guidelines.
- As is usual, do remember to record your concerns, decisions made and actions taken in your case notes. It is important that you contact your supervisor or one of the Senior Counsellors as soon as possible to talk this situation through with them.

Do make sure that you always keep at hand a full list of services on campus and useful phone numbers.

We do sometimes see clients who express concerns about a housemate, friend or colleague on campus. We can support them but they may need to seek help from the emergency services if the situation becomes serious.

Case Story of Esther – Suicidal Feelings

Esther was in the third year of her course studying English and German. She had taken a year out to see if that could help her deep feelings of guilt and shame that had plagued her most of her life and long-term thoughts and fantasies of suicide. It had been a good year for her, she had travelled around Europe with a friend, she'd worked on beaches in Greece in the summer, she'd climbed mountains in Germany, Spain and France. She was good at languages, and this had all helped her to relax as much as she was able, which was not easy for her. She'd kept a diary and enjoyed the process of writing. But, now here she was back at university for her final year, and things were not good for her.

I asked what she wanted from the counselling.

> I thought coming back to university, I would feel better. I've done a lot of things I wanted to do. But, when good things happen to me, it sometimes makes me feel guilty, as if I just don't deserve it, which makes me feel ashamed

I asked if she had any idea where those feelings had come from.

"I don't, but those feelings have always been there as long as I can remember".

"Can you tell me about those feelings?"

"My earliest memories, are of a sense that I have done something wrong, but I don't know what it is".

"Was there anything else going on in your family that may have caused feelings of guilt or shame?" "Well, I don't often think about it but I remember being told that I should feel very fortunate, by my grandmother, because I had survived and my younger brother had died in a flu epidemic, where we lived"

"She will occasionally say, she wishes my brother, Thomas, was still alive". "Sometimes, when she says that, it makes me feel that I am somehow responsible and that maybe she doesn't want me to be here".

> My parents don't really talk about him and there are no photos of him up in the house. It feels like a family secret. I don't ask about it. I don't want to cause them pain. I think it has made me feel guilty and somehow ashamed that I have survived and he didn't. My grandmother would talk about him to me, occasionally but I feel she almost resented me for being here instead of Thomas.

"How old were you when he died?"

> I was three and I think he was about 10 months old when he died. I remember holding him and playing with him, but I don't have very clear memories of him. I do remember my mum and dad crying and it was kind of scary and 'wrong' somehow.

"I think I felt sort of guilty and careful around my parents".

"I think that there is a weird kind of guilt in me for surviving and sometimes I imagine that they would prefer that he was here, rather than me".

"How does that make you feel now Esther?"

"I do think his death is connected to my feelings of guilt and shame".

"Have you talked to your parents about how you feel?"

"No, I haven't wanted to hurt them by bringing it up".

> It's always made me feel that I have to behave well and perform at a higher level to make up for my brother dying. I can see that, this whole thing may have contributed to me feeling, that I shouldn't be here either. When I've felt very down, I have thought of taking an overdose, several times.

Esther's eyes filled with tears.

"That must have felt terrible for you and a real pressure".

"How would you feel about talking to your parents about this now? It feels as if you have been protecting them from your feelings". "They may not realise how you have been feeling. You can't take away their pain and grief, that is not your responsibility".

"I just don't want to cause them to feel guilty about me".

> Maybe it will help them to know how you feel, after all, you have all of you lost an important member of your family. Perhaps you could, all together, think of some positive way of honouring his short life. That might actually help take any pressure off of your shoulders. It feels as if you have been carrying this weight for a long time.

Esther really cried, but it felt like a real letting go of the weight of her guilt and shame for 'being alive'. She remembered feeling she had to always be 'good' to somehow make up for her brother having died. Over the years, she had occasionally felt a real sense of desolation and emptiness. She had thought seriously of suicide when she felt particularly down, but she didn't want to cause her parents more pain.

I suggested that maybe she could buy herself some kind of memento for having been a 'survivor', she smiled for the first time.

Esther went home in the half-term and asked to talk to both of her parents; luckily her grandmother was staying with other family, so she had a good opportunity to talk to them on their own. They talked together for a long time, and both of her parents were devastated to realise what effect their grief and loss of their son had been having on Esther. They showed her a small pair of shoes, a blue baby suit and a bib that had belonged to Thomas, which she had not seen before. They had wanted to protect her but this had exacerbated her guilt. They spent some time grieving together, and they talked about Thomas and how well she had played with him, little stories, she had not heard before. They apologised for not involving her in their grief. When she came back to the counselling, she knew it would take a long time, but she felt a healing process happening in herself for the loss of Thomas, and also for the loss of her relationship with her parents. It felt as if they had cut her out of 'their shared' loss. For her, it had not just been the loss of her brother but also the loss of a part of her parents. They had had the best intentions, to protect her, but it had also made her feel shut out, and she had developed a real feeling of 'guilt' and 'shame' about that.

Suicide

One of the worst experiences for us as counsellors is when a client commits suicide. It is always disturbing, and there can be a lot of guilt about not having been able to stop this from happening. The relationship we have with our clients is important and when such things happen, it is distressing and very sad. We are using ourselves as a tool, but even with our professional boundaries in place, we can't do this work without being engaged in the relationship we form with our clients with our hearts as well as our heads. This is when our individual supervision and our group supervision are so very helpful. However, we may also need extra support from colleagues, friends and sometimes from some counselling for ourselves too.

Supervision with Helen, a Counsellor, Whose Client Had Committed Suicide

Helen was a very experienced counsellor who had been working with Graham for a couple of months. He had originally come for counselling for depression, which he had been living with for most of his life. He couldn't really remember a time when he didn't feel depressed. He saw his doctor regularly and was taking antidepressants. He had had periods of psychotherapy and had psychiatric help over about five years, after two suicide attempts with drugs and alcohol at 18 and 21. The second attempt had been more serious.

He was coming into the last term of his third year studying a Ph.D. in physics, when he began counselling with Helen. He was feeling particularly down about 'what next'. His academic work had gone really well. His research had been very successful, and there were many options for him in terms of work. He had quite a few opportunities and choices about jobs, and had even thought of continuing in academia.

He had always been a high achiever and expected to do really well in his exams. But his depression had quite often got worse over the years when he was successful. He was very aware of this. He had a deep feeling of 'being a bad person', with no real evidence for feeling like that. His family had always been supportive. But he often felt guilty, but had no idea what that was about. Sometimes, he would just feel he had done something so wrong, but couldn't remember what it might have been. He had had conversations with his parents, and none of it made sense to them as to why he felt like this. They told him that other than normal arguments with his two sisters and his brother, he had always been very caring, hard-working and just a pleasure to have around. They were puzzled as to why he felt like this about himself. He'd had quite a lot of psychiatric help, but nothing had ever really convinced him that he wasn't 'trouble' to other people, in some way.

Helen was worried about him; she saw a change in his depression, which seemed worse. He had sought advice from his doctor and was taking a higher dose of his antidepressants. But as he was approaching finishing his dissertation, which was going well, he seemed to get lower and lower in mood.

Helen had checked with him about any fears of going out into the world. He was a very astute young man and he admitted that this was a kind of crossroads for him. Helen was a very intuitive counsellor and she was becoming more and more worried about him. She suggested he go back to see his psychiatrist, whom he had worked with well over time, for a review of his 'suicidal feelings' and his overall medication, and Graham agreed. Helen was relieved but she felt that the idea of ending education and going out into the 'adult' world was feeling like 'a step too far for him'. She had asked him directly if he felt suicidal. He had cried and told her that he felt helpless about those feelings. He told her that he knew he was so fortunate with his studies, his family and he had a new girlfriend whom he was pretty keen on. He didn't understand why he felt so down sometimes. He told her, he sometimes felt a weird inner guilt as if in the past, he had done something so awful. It made him feel that when good things happened, it was just 'wrong', that he hadn't 'paid for' whatever it was.

Helen was worried about him because this feeling seemed so genuine and real in him. She was reassured that he would be seeing his psychiatrist. He made an appointment with her a week after he was due to see his psychiatrist.

Graham never turned up to that appointment, and instead she heard from the medical centre that he had committed suicide. He had gone for a walk down by the sea, not far away, had cut his wrists and had been found dead in the early morning by a walker. Helen had gone to his funeral, which had been held locally. His parents had searched her out and they could not have been nicer people. It was tragic.

We had booked a supervision, this time just to talk about how Helen was feeling about his death. She was very upset but after the funeral, she also, strangely, felt almost a relief for him. She realised there was a tortured part of him that, from his descriptions of his early life, had been tearing him apart in some way, as long as he could remember. It genuinely didn't feel as if it was to do with his family or his upbringing.

It almost felt to her that, maybe whatever had been torturing him, might even have come from 'a past life'. We both agreed there are some things that just don't always make sense. Whatever the cause was, it was helpful for Helen to express some of her feelings of failure, of not having been able to prevent Graham killing himself. There was certainly, for her, a sense of guilt, a sense of having let Graham down, which we both agreed needed releasing. There is nothing anyone can do to stop someone from committing suicide, if that is their choice. This was very hard for Helen.

Helen had taken a week off from work, to deal with her feelings. It is one of the most difficult situations, as a counsellor, to have to accept that for some people it is an option, a choice, to take their lives. Some emotional pain can be just unbearable, unexplainable and sometimes too much to live with. Helen needed a break to come to terms with this. We continued to talk about this a few times in our regular supervision and Helen was supported by our regular departmental supervision. It was certainly not the first time this had happened within the counselling service or within the university, but fortunately it is still a rarity.

Chapter 19

Surviving Rape and Sexual Abuse

A Hidden Scar

Surviving Rape

Every year, as a counsellor, I worked with many clients, most often women, but occasionally men, who had been raped, assaulted or attacked in some way either in their childhood, adolescence or more recently as adults. Mostly this would have been by complete strangers but occasionally this was by adults whom they had trusted. Hardly any clients I worked with have reported such a wounding experience to the police or anyone else. Each situation is uniquely different and exceptionally painful. It can happen to anyone, may involve varying degrees of violence and is traumatic and humiliating, leaving deep scars in the person whose body, freedom of choice and personal space have been violated.

As counsellors, we listen to our clients in a way that we're really meeting them and hearing their experiences and even though we may have heard many such stories, it is always shocking to be with someone who has experienced this kind of trauma. This is why as counsellors, we need to 'debrief' in our own regular supervision and peer case discussions. The fact that we are familiar with such stories can make it easier for clients to tell us what has happened. We are more able to normalise, 'that bad things happen', because they do! It hasn't happened to our clients because they have done something wrong; such attacks are usually random and opportunistic but there are people who search out work with children and young people who use their positions to abuse children and young people.

I believe one of the most difficult situations is when sexual abuse takes place in a family and is never spoken about or dealt with. This is the hardest situation for many children to recover from. The lack of trust, safety and the annihilation of boundaries within the family is one of the most difficult abuses for anyone to recover from. It is the one place where it would be expected that there is safety, but of course, sometimes, this is just not true. As counsellors, it is very hard to listen to accounts of childhood sexual abuse but counselling really can gradually help our clients to recover from this childhood trauma. I have often seen clients show enormous courage and be determined to recover. Young people can be very resilient, and it is inspiring to see that strength in people shine through and enable them to put the abuse behind them in adulthood.

DOI: 10.4324/9781003754244-21

It would be wonderful if we lived in an idyllic world without violence, abuse, power struggles, the need to control and hurt other people, but we don't. There may be occasions when a client hasn't picked up on 'something' and were not sufficiently protective of themselves, but the truth is that people who rape, bully and abuse become very adept at what they do and are usually highly motivated to do so. What is important is how we can support survivors of rape and abuse to recover from the pain and humiliation of such abuse.

Some clients need to tell us what has happened to them, while other people don't want to talk about the trauma itself but want to talk about how they feel now and how they can move on. Other clients may simply want more practical advice. Usually, by the time our clients see a counsellor, they have already made a decision about reporting their experiences to the police or not. Many clients believe that it is not only futile, but they would be risking further distress if they report their abuse to the police.

However, there are members of the police who are very well trained to specifically deal with these situations. One of the biggest problems is the extremely personal nature of such crimes, and the idea of discussing what may have happened to the police or worse still, in a court of law, can be devastating for many people. This is, sadly, why most clients I have worked with would never have considered going to the police to report such an attack or abuse.

This makes what we can do in the counselling so much more important in trying to help people who have experienced rape or sexual abuse to recover as much as they can. Some clients want to consider options for punishment of the perpetrator and may decide to report the incident in a limited way; others may wait or join with other people if it becomes known that others have received similar treatment from the same person, at a later date.

Sometimes, as time goes on, the shock of what has happened can be acknowledged, assimilated and integrated into something the client has survived. In time, I have seen people recover their sense of power and their trust in themselves having coped with something truly horrible, but it can take much longer to gain back trust 'in the World'. For some, fear can become a nightmarish companion for weeks, months and even years later, flashbacks are common, and that wonderfully innocent sense of safety, security and trust in the world, which we often don't appreciate until we have lost it, may be buried for good. Time, good support and a courageous willingness to risk new experiences of going out into the world may help to rebuild confidence and trust again.

Some clients find it helpful to write down an account of what has happened to them, to help them to come to terms with the reality of it. Other clients prefer to write a letter (which they don't send) to their attacker saying what they would like to have said to them or telling them how it has affected them. It can be empowering, and very real, if a client chooses to read this out, in the form of a role-play by putting the attacker in the 'empty chair'.

This is a simple visualisation/relaxation, which some people find useful. Sitting in their chair, take some deep breaths in and out until they are feeling more relaxed, taking their time. The client is asked to imagine the healing, restoring and strengthening of the personal space and personal boundaries around their body, including the healing of any wounds they sustained. It is important for them to breathe slowly in and out, imagining their breath bringing in healing to every part of their body, but especially a sense of being washed clean with every breath they take in.

For some clients, just talking about what has happened can help people to begin to release some of the trauma of such an experience and recover their equilibrium and perspective again, especially talking to a professional counsellor or therapist who is used to hearing such experiences.

Many people are reluctant to share the realities of such traumatic experiences with family or friends for fear of distressing them. I would stress that getting therapeutic help and support can truly enable people to survive, recover and regain their ability to have trust in the world again.

Case Story of Brian – Rape

There's a lecturer he's afraid of. He's behind in his work. He's quiet, withdrawn. He talks about his fear of this man, his fear of failure. He did reasonably well in his first and second years, but he just hasn't settled into this important third year, and he is getting behind in his work. He's got a few friends and interests that he takes part in but he's not really 'here'.

It is a few weeks into the counselling. I feel he is kind of testing out the counselling. There is something more going on with Brian. As I greet him, he seems especially anxious. There is something heavy in the room. He sits quietly and his eyes well up. He begins to sob and shake.

His words lurch into the room.

> "I was 17, on holiday with two friends. I had a bit to drink. It was getting dark. I clamber up onto the sand dunes to pee. This man comes up behind me, traps my hands, pushes a cloth into my mouth. I can't move, he pulls my shorts down, bends me over, drills himself into me. The pain tears my insides and consumes me. He's fast, efficient, terrifying. He's a blur of violence".

"He runs off leaving his brutality, his stench, his cloth in my mouth. I pull up my shorts. I'm bleeding, shaking uncontrollably. I fall onto the sand, can't move. I throw up and feel ice cold".

> "I force myself to get up, shout to my friends that I'm going back to the caravan. I make it into the shower block. I stand under the shower as long as I can bear it. In slow motion. I stumble back to the caravan, dry myself. I crawl into my sleeping bag. I can't stop shaking. I vow I will never tell anyone what happened. I pretend to be asleep when my mates come back".

I tell Brian how sorry I am that this happened to him. I tell him how brave it is for him to be able to tell me and face up to the horror of this happening to him. I tell Brian that this is such a hard and painful thing for anyone to share, to relive.

> "I've never told anyone until today. It was so fast. It was just so fast. I feel the humiliation everywhere inside me still. I feel guilty. Why couldn't I stop him? Why did he do this to me? The pain, the smell, the taste, the sounds have never left me. I force it down, but the smallest thing can take me back. I couldn't tell anyone about this. This makes it real, this really did happen to me".

In the counselling, gradually, Brian began to accept that this was something that had happened **to** him, not something he invited or had any choice about. This shadowy man was an expert at rape as many rapists are.

He expressed the shock, the fear and the impotence, but there was a degree of separation, and gradually he had begun the process of letting it go. It didn't come from him. It didn't have to stay with him. The hardest feelings to overcome were the humiliation and the guilt that he had not been able to fight back, that he had not been able to stop this happening to him.

I asked if he had ever thought of reporting it. He immediately shook his head. "How could I". "It would just feel like being raped all over again".

It took a long time for him to even begin to come to terms with what had happened to him. It is hard for men and women to talk about rape. The rape of men is less publicised and can be less understood. It is easy to be paralysed by such a terrible abuse. An experienced rapist can rape a man, woman or child very fast. They know exactly what they are doing, have probably done it many times, and they know that the shock of it can freeze and shock the person they are abusing.

I really honoured Brian's courage to share this in the counselling. He gradually seemed visually less pale and less tense in our subsequent sessions. After several sessions, I asked him what would help him now. He told me he felt lighter, just having admitted how much it had hurt him. I asked if there was anything else that might help release this even more. He felt so very angry that this man was probably continuing to do this and nothing would happen to him.

Brian came up with the idea of him drawing a picture of this man on a piece of paper and burning it. It would help him to let go of some of his deep anger.

The next session, he came looking a little bit lighter. He told me he had waited until his housemates were all out. He had already drawn several pictures of the perpetrator and he had ripped them up, but it was more powerful this night he had drawn a few blurry images of this man and had set fire to them in a flower pot in the garden of his student house. He then imagined the man floating away into the air with the smoke. It brought up some deep anger, and he was able to let some of it out, punching his pillow. It felt like a release of sorts. The man's image became blurry for him. He seemed to be disappearing from his thinking. Brian felt less helpless.

He still felt he needed something more to get back a part of him that felt 'missing'. Especially his sexuality. He had not had any physical or sexual contact with anyone since then. He'd been afraid to ask any woman out on a date. It made him question his sexuality, his ability to have sex or even feel any sexual feelings. Those feelings felt dead inside him. This bought up in him a deep sadness, which he was able to express and talk about in the counselling.

We talked about what might help and I asked if he would be up for having a massage, maybe beginning with a session of reflexology, just to begin to get a sense of positive human touch in his feet, something that might enable him to feel positive about his body again. He wasn't sure if he was ready for that yet.

Then, the next week he came into the room with a slight smile. He had been very brave indeed and had booked a reflexology foot massage in town with a woman who was quite a bit older and seemed very kind. He really liked her and although it had felt weird at first, he found himself relaxing and talking to the woman who was doing it. He didn't tell her anything about what had happened to him, but he had felt 'safe'. He decided that he would do it on a regular basis for a while to help him get back the feelings in his body. It felt okay that it was his feet and he realised, it would take quite a while to even feel his whole body again. He still felt, 'kind of frozen'.

I congratulated him for being so very brave. I really admired him for wanting to get back his sense of self and get back the feelings in his body. It had been a terrible experience and would still take him a long time to recover from but he'd been very brave indeed. We worked together for another two months, and Brian was determined to recover from such a violent and horrible experience.

Chapter 20

Trauma and Post-Traumatic Stress Disorder

Stuck in the Past

When we experience trauma in our lives, either physical or emotional trauma, our bodies can often go into deep shock, the trauma experienced can be extreme or at a low level which can go almost unnoticed. What is important is that after a trauma such as an accident, bereavement, attack, rape, childhood sexual abuse, near-death experience, natural disaster we get support from friends and professional help. It may be that we are not directly involved but are a witness to such an event, but we may still suffer from traumatic stress. Human beings are sensitive to trauma, and there are some people so sensitive that they can even be traumatised by events they see on film and television and they would be wise to limit their viewing. Post-traumatic stress disorder (PTSD) can sometimes be accumulative and this is well recognised by the armed forces and emergency services whose staff are prime candidates for PTSD.

There has been much discussion as to the best time for any professional intervention after a particular trauma. Some people want to talk about what has happened to them immediately afterwards, for others it may take a year or longer before they are able to speak about a particular trauma. Sometimes survivors of childhood physical, emotional or sexual abuse have actually blocked from their mind such abuse, but may begin to get 'flashbacks' only when they are in a strong and safe enough position as an adult for their unconscious to allow them to remember such trauma. The effects of deep trauma may be expressed in different ways, fears, panic attacks and phobias, nightmares, problems sleeping, difficulty in concentrating, racing heart beats, feeling disconnected from yourself or other people, negative thoughts, anger, guilt, excess sweating, shakiness or feeling jumpy, hyper-vigilance, avoidance of certain situations, I would say that each one of us would be unique in our reactions to trauma. It can be extremely helpful for anyone experiencing trauma to seek professional counselling.

DOI: 10.4324/9781003754244-22

Case Story of Ravi – PTSD

Ravi is a second-year student, normally a high achieving student enjoying his law degree. He is finding it difficult to focus on his course this year. During the summer break he was coming home from a night out with friends in the early hours and he witnessed a terrible accident. He described a Skoda Fabia driving past him at high speed and as it went round a bend in the road ahead, there was an almighty crash as it smashed into a large truck parked up at the side of the road. The sound was shocking with the breaking of glass, steel into steel and worst of all were the screams which carried on afterwards for what seemed ages. He ran towards it. There was a complete mess of metal in the road. One boy had shot straight through the windscreen and lay crumpled and unmoving in the road. The driver was trapped in the crushed front of the car and was almost certainly dead. Screams were coming from the backseat where there was a young girl. with lots of blood on the side of her head and he tried to comfort her as he phoned the emergency services. A couple approached the man lying in the road from a nearby house. Ravi climbed into the space next to the young girl but felt helpless to know what to do. He took off his jumper and tried to keep her warm and used something in the car to stem one of her wounds which was bleeding heavily on the side of her head. He just kept talking to her. She quietened but was shaking uncontrollably and was very cold. She began to whimper as the blue lights came into view of an ambulance and a police car. They rushed to help as he eased himself out of what was left of the car.

There was little anyone could do; the two young men, aged 14 and 15 had both died instantly. They took the girl to hospital but there was nothing they could do for her. She died of head and chest injuries. She was just 14 years old.

He had been very shaken up for a week or so but then got on with his life. On coming back to university this term, he began to have nightmares, flashbacks and began to shake uncontrollably quite randomly. He went to see the doctor at the medical centre who suggested he come for some counselling.

Ravi was tall, direct and noticeably nervous. I noticed his upper lip was sweaty and his hands were shaking. He hadn't really talked about the accident much with his family or friends. He didn't want to burden them with it. He was accustomed to being quite independent.

He said it felt difficult initially and a bit embarrassing to talk about it all but it was also a relief. He felt the horror of the whole thing was living inside him. As he spoke about the young girl, his eyes filled with tears. He kept apologising for his feelings and said this whole thing had confused him. He didn't understand why he had felt so churned up. He talked of feeling that he had suddenly 'gone to pieces' after getting back to university. He was beginning to feel almost scared of going to sleep in case he woke up in the middle of the night sweating and shaking uncontrollably. He kept reliving it again and again. He had such vivid images of himself holding the young girl who died, whose name was Kylie. Sometimes, he would imagine his younger sister in the car instead of Kylie; his sister was also 14. He'd always felt rather protective of her.

What made him go and see the doctor was that he was beginning to have panic attacks during the day as well, out of the blue, for no apparent reason. It was a new and uncomfortable feeling for him, feeling so out of control. He was fairly against taking pills from the doctor, so when she suggested his coming for counselling, he was prepared to come and see if it would help.

Ravi was very honest about having to overcome his shame about what he perceived as his 'being weak'. He was the oldest son in his family and had always been a high achiever and strong, which had somehow made all this worse for him.

There were three things that made this situation particularly difficult for Ravi. First, there was the extreme trauma, shock and utter horror of witnessing such a terrible and violent accident. He had bottled up some of what he had seen and didn't want to talk about it and upset his family and friends. Secondly, he had never witnessed anything like that before, and it was the speed with which it all happened. One minute he was happily walking along on a familiar road home after a pleasant evening with friends and suddenly it felt he was thrown into sounds and sights of devastation and death, everything broken. This is playing out in nightmares as he wakes up in a sweat and shaking with recurring images of what had happened and has shaken his confidence and trust in going out at night, which is totally understandable. Thirdly, he had never experienced such helpless feelings before. As the oldest son, he often felt he had to be the strong and successful one, not wanting to let his parents and family down. Some of his flashbacks are focussed on his feelings of helplessness, of not being able to do anything to help Kylie. Although he had been born in the UK, his parents had come to the UK not long before he was born, as refugees. They were quite a tight family with no grandparents here and he felt a pressure to do well, be helpful and be a high achiever. He was also quite protective of his sister when there had been some racist comments at her school. He was very upset at not having been able to help this young girl, Kylie. He had felt afraid of doing the wrong thing and had felt so utterly helpless.

It really helped Ravi to talk about what had happened and realise how much he had helped by phoning for help and by getting involved and doing his best to comfort Kylie in a terrible situation. He had actually been very strong. It can be hard to come to terms with such an extreme traumatic event, happening out of the blue. It helped him to do some breathing exercises that he could use when he experienced waking in the night or flashbacks.

Ravi came back for a final half-hour third session, just to check in. He used this session to talk about some of the other pressures he had been feeling, before the accident, of having expectations of his family on him as the oldest son of a family making a new life in a new country and what that meant to him. He had never really talked about this before. It was also an opportunity for Ravi to value his strengths and allow himself to be vulnerable.

He had carried on doing the breathing exercises, because they generally enabled him to relax. He felt he was able to deal with the occasional flashbacks that he was still experiencing. He realised he had been able to help Kylie by being there for her. He still felt sad and shocked by the terrible death of three young people in such a horrible way. He couldn't get over how fast it had all happened. I asked him what would give him closure.

He decided that he wanted to go to a local church and light a candle for each one of the young people who had died. It felt to him like something he could do to let go of the whole experience in a positive way. We left it that he could come back for a follow up session if he needed it.

Part 3

Groupwork – A Group for Refugees

Finding Your Place and Honouring Your Journey Here

This was a six-week group, meeting for two hours per week. It was originally designed to help a particular group of refugees, but it could also be adapted to any overseas students who have newly arrived in the UK, or any group of students who have newly arrived on campus. It was hoped that participants would grow in self-awareness, self-esteem and assertiveness skills. It was hoped that they would use this group to gain confidence and find support to enable them to find their place at university and here in the UK with more ease. Each session begins with a check in at the beginning and includes a relaxation or a visualisation at the end. Ground rules of timing and confidentiality were agreed in the group.

Week 1 – Introduction

It would be good to give out a book and pen to each person in the group. But, reassure them they don't have to share it, it really is for them to keep to acknowledge their own journey here.

Tell us: something about your name, something about yourself and where you began your life.

Tell us: what you want to achieve for yourself here at university.

Differences in culture can be confusing, but also fun – a certain obsession in the UK with saying please and thank you; in Holland and Germany you don't ask someone if you can sit in between them on a train you just gesture with your hand to 'shift up';

Tell us: something that is distinctive about your own culture?

Tell us: what was positive about arriving here in the UK?

Tell us: what has been difficult?

Ask group members to complete this hand-out below. Allow ten minutes. Ask them to discuss the results with someone else in the group five to ten minutes each. They might want to share something in the main group, depending on the size of the group.

Where Do I Want to Be?

What would you like to be doing in two years' time?

DOI: 10.4324/9781003754244-23

What would you like to be doing in five years' time?

It can help us to reach our goals and ideals by the use of visualisation or 'putting out an intention' into the world and in the process naming our intentions to ourselves. List your ideal goals, what you want to achieve in each of these three main life areas below:

CAREER:

PERSONAL LIFE:

PERSONAL FULFILMENT:

Choose one of these, close your eyes and visualise yourself being in this position in every minute detail. Have fun with it and if you picture yourself in a room, describe the room in detail to yourself: colours, shapes, smells and even tastes. Imagine the people around you in detail. Make this visualisation really come alive for you. You could do this for each of your goals. Then, with a group member, you could discuss what steps you need to make to reach these goals, thinking up small changes initially which could put you further on down the track you want to be on. Whenever we choose to move forward positively in one area of our life it has a positive effect on other aspects of our lives. Depending on the size of the group and timing, some people may want to share this in the group as a whole.

End with a 15-Minute Relaxation

Think of a place where you feel totally safe, it may be out in nature somewhere or in a favourite place, real or imagined. This needs to be a place you can go back to any time in your mind, a safe place to relax and be yourself. Notice the colours, shapes, sounds, plants, trees and smells that help to connect you strongly to this place.

Take a few deep breaths deep into your lungs and lengthen your out-breath. Allow your breathing to return to normal. Notice yourself being held by the chair, this place, the Earth beneath you supporting you. Feel what it is to be held and supported in a safe place.

Run through your body and imagine breathing in stillness to each part of your body: toes, feet, ankles, lower legs, knees, upper legs, all of your legs from hips to tip of your toes and breathe in stillness. Move to fingers, hands, wrists, lower arm, elbows, upper arms, all of your arms from shoulder to tip of the fingers and breath in stillness. Move to your lower body, bottom, stomach, chest and breathe in stillness. Move to your neck, chin, mouth, face, eyes, ears, hair, scalp, all of your head from neck to top of your head and breath in stillness. Notice again, your whole self, feeling held and supported by your chair, by yourself.

Find the place where your heart is and imagine your heart smiling, simply smiling. Stay with this image and then slowly, in your own time come back into this room, into this space and notice a colour or shape in this room to ground yourself back here. Allow yourself to feel safe to really be present here in this group.

Homework: Notice how you talk to your self this week. Are you hard on yourself or encouraging?

Week 2 – Support from Inside

It is very important for us to support ourselves, and how we feel about ourselves is affected by how we speak to ourselves. It is therefore important to build a good relationship with ourselves as much as we can. This really is our best support that helps us cope and helps us live our lives in the best possible ways. We need to create positive messages and beliefs about ourself, encourage ourselves and make good decisions about how we treat ourselves. We truly need to be our own best friend.

CHECK IN: What did you notice about your self-talk this past week?

What Is Self-Esteem?

As we arrive in adulthood, our level of self-esteem reflects how nurturing and supportive the people around us were. The way our parents, teachers, family and friends regard, judge, love, value, respect and behave towards us helps to create how we regard, judge, love, value, respect or behave towards ourselves. This includes people who have social, cultural and political power over our well-being. None of these people exists in a vacuum, so their behaviour towards us will have been influenced by their own experiences, beliefs, cultural, religious, political and social norms. So, we receive messages about ourselves from many different people for many different reasons but that doesn't make them true and such messages **'are not set in stone!'**

We may not have had control of how other people viewed and treated us but we can take control of our future view and treatment of ourselves. We can choose to get to know our strengths, skills and positive aspects, and we can choose to build on these and learn to love, approve, accept and care for ourselves the best we can.

For many of us self-esteem takes a pounding during the process of childhood, especially given the pressures that exist in schools, family life and in Society as a whole. There is much emphasis placed on 'performance'. There is pressure to achieve at younger and younger ages: goals and grades; assessments and inspections. Children have become highly measured commodities. The fear, uncertainty, self-doubt and negativity which can be generated by such a system can be a breeding ground for low self-esteem. Many of us have learnt to exaggerate our mistakes and excel at self-doubt and self-criticism. Many children are having to deal with the stress and trauma of poverty, loss and separation, abuse, ill health and the results of war.

How can we turn this around and build self-esteem. It is a freedom for us to emphasise what we **are** achieving, what we **are** capable of, what we **are** doing well and how loveable and amazing we **are**. Challenges, change, mistakes and crises are a part of each of our lives, and it is from such experiences that we learn our best coping strategies and become aware of our many human strengths and abilities. We need appreciation for this from ourselves and from other people. It helps us to build confidence in ourselves if we acknowledge our strengths and positive skills, at least to ourselves!

Building Self-Esteem

One of the major tasks for us as maturing adults is to become wise, and it is wise for us to build the best possible relationship with ourselves. Some of us have high self-esteem in some areas of our lives and maybe not in others. To feel good about ourselves leads us to be powerful in our lives and can help us to transform out-dated negative beliefs and behaviours into positive beliefs and behaviours. As we increase our self-esteem and our confidence to do things better, it builds on itself! If you nurture and feed a plant it grows strong and healthy and produces the best flowers and fruit. We are the same. We become much more able to develop talents and gifts to take out into the world - we blossom!

The first step of regaining self-esteem is to notice how we talk to ourselves. Sometimes I have worked with clients in counselling, and I notice that they have used the word 'stupid' about themselves several times in the first ten minutes of the counselling. Often people are really surprised about this when it is pointed out to them. I've noticed too the number of times we may all say, 'I can't'. This can be disempowering and is often untrue. It helps us to become aware of how we speak to and about ourselves.

The most important relationship in our life, the longest lasting and most intimate is our relationship with ourself. In our relationship with ourself we are constantly talking to ourself. It helps us to notice how we speak to ourself, how we speak about ourself to other people, how we treat ourself, how we feel about ourself. Notice whether we can be more positive towards ourself. We all need love, support and encouragement. We all need to become our own best friend. When this relationship is good, other relationships, our life in general, runs more smoothly! We need to emphasise our strengths, the things we do well and what we like about ourself. We need to promote ourself to ourself and to the world in the same way that we would a friend.

Building a Solid Centre

One way we can build a solid centre inside ourself is to imagine a tall solid tower running through the centre of our bodies from our feet to the top of our head, made of bricks. Every time we do something positive for ourselves: reward ourself for something we have done well; buy ourself a treat; visit somewhere we've always wanted to visit; phone a friend who encourages us; do something that gives us joy – listen to lovely music, read something that inspires us, buy a single flower to admire, take time to walk somewhere beautiful, visit an art exhibition which inspires us, make ourself a lovely meal. Imagine that this adds a solid brick to that tall internal tower, strengthening us at our very centre. Then, imagine that when we do something that harms ourself: put ourself down, put up with something or some-one harms us. For example, if we are eating too much, too little drinking too much alcohol, so that we feel bad, hoard too many things around us so that our space is uncomfortable. This takes a brick out of that centre and weakens the strength and power of that brick tower which can make us feel more vulnerable and weaker in our very centre. Then think of more positive things to do. The more commitment we make to ourself, the better we will feel. We are worth it!

Affirmations

It can be helpful for us to use affirmations. If we think of a positive statement that is the opposite of how we might normally think about ourself and just say it over and over again to ourself as we are walking along, as we are waiting in a queue. When we do this and notice what happens in our body, we can feel a lightness of step, a lift of energy. Just as when we smile or laugh it has a real 'feel good' effect. By using positive statements, we can re-programme new messages into our self-awareness and consciousness, which can build our self-esteem.

It can be helpful to give a few minutes to think about what we are grateful for about ourself. Gratitude about our many gifts, good health and well-being is a vital part of moving forward positively. We could buy a special card, with a picture that we identify with in some way and write in it a list of things we enjoy about ourself and keep adding to it. How much better it would be to fall asleep at night, thinking of a few positive things we have done that day. Often, we can be good at dwelling on any negatives but the positive things might make you fall asleep with a smile on your face!

You may like to choose one of the following positive statements to say to yourself a few dozen times. You could breathe it in slowly as you are sitting in a relaxed place or just before you go to sleep. Notice how your energy levels change. Keep doing it, even if it sounds awkward at first.

Positive Statements to Begin with, Until You Create Your Own!

I can handle anything that comes my way
I trust myself and I trust the process of life
Life is sweet and so am I
I welcome risks that expand my life
All is well inside and outside of me
I know this (meeting/seminar/presentation/interview) will go well
I belong in the world as an equal
I am loving myself more each day
I recognise my own successes
I am alive to joy, play and laughter.
I am powerful and I love it

It can take effort and work to regain a realistic and positive perception of ourselves. If we allow ourselves to know and recognise what we are good at and realise our potential in different aspects of our lives, then we may begin to recognise what a gift we are to the world and then we may take our rightful space.

Tell us: about two of your strengths, things you like about yourself, in the main group.

Discuss: with someone else in the group, what messages or beliefs would be useful to help you to increase your self-esteem?

Tell us: about two of your skills, things you are good at, in the main group.

Discuss: with someone different in the group what messages or beliefs would help you increase your confidence in the skills you have.

Notice when you are wanting to achieve something, how differently you feel when you say over and over to yourself, "I can do this", "I can do this", "I can do this". It really does make a difference, and sometimes it can be effective to shut our eyes, and just imagine that we are doing, whatever it is. This is often the basis of training, which can improve performance in sportsmen and sportswomen.

So many children arrive in adulthood unable to believe that they can sing, dance, play a musical instrument, write, paint, learn a language. Those beliefs can be changed. So many of us are simply afraid of getting it wrong. We also need to learn to accept how important mistakes are in helping us, eventually, to get it right!

In order to support ourselves, we need the most positive messages and beliefs about our strengths, skills and about the fact that we deserve to be successful. I like the statement from writer, Maya Angelou, who defined success as, "liking yourself, liking what you do and liking how you do it".

Can you think of a positive statement for yourself to focus on during this coming week about yourself or about something you are good at?

We Will End With A 15-Minute Relaxation

It would be great if you could begin this relaxation with a journey through your whole body, guided by you, starting at the top of your head, imagining a bright warm light resting gently on your head. You are going to guide this warm light, slowly throughout your body, taking it at your own pace, gently, into and around each and every part of your body. As this light gently moves around you, feel its soft energy permeate every part of you wherever you want to take it. It is your choice where and how you choose to do this, knowing you have 15 minutes to enjoy this experience you are giving to yourself. May you encourage yourself to feel replenished in a way that is right for you so that you can fully relax and be present to yourself during this time. You are fully in charge of giving this time and space to yourself in the very best possible way that works for you. Enjoy!

Homework: For next week think about people and situations where you get your best support from.

Week 3 – Support from Outside

Can you think about people who you feel really have supported you, from your family, friends, people in this group, teachers you have or have had connections with? Are there new skills you've learnt that support you? Can you assert yourself or ask for help from others? Is there advice or information that has helped you in your life? Are there stories and experiences from other people that have helped you to grow, learn and feel supported? Could you make a list of books, websites, films, blogs, anything else that has supported you.

CHECK IN: Do you feel you deserve support from other people and can you ask for it, when needed?

Tell us: do you feel that you deserve to have support from others?

Tell us: can you ask for what you need and want?

Assertiveness

Assertiveness is connected with how you stand, an assertive pose, facing squarely on and having your feet evenly spaced on the floor, looking someone in the eye. You can try out a passive pose and an aggressive pose, and what is in the middle of those two is your assertive pose. Feel it in your body; it is a strong, steady stance. A position it is easy to stand in for some time and be comfortable. Try all three poses, it is fun to test them out and experience which one feels more stable. You could practice it in pairs, in your group.

Part of receiving support from outside is being able to give support to others, mutual support. It increases our sense of belonging to any group when we both accept support and give support. In helping others, we can become more confident. Knowing we can care for others increases our sense of competence and well-being. It just feels good.

I'm Okay, You're Okay

As you sit in your chair, imagine that feeling of, 'I'm okay and You're okay' that you need to have when being assertive. Imagine facing a past, present or future situation where you needed or will need to have this. Feel it in every part of you. It is so much easier to feel positive about other people if you have positive feelings about yourself. This makes it easier for you to be assertive. If you feel on an equal footing with other people, there is mutual respect, which makes it easier to ask for advice or help.

Visualisation

Find a balanced, strong and comfortable position in your body, fill your chair and imagine that feeling of, 'I'm Okay and You're Okay', a feeling you need in your whole body when being assertive. Imagine facing a past, present or future situation where you needed or will need to have this and use it to ask for something for yourself. Feel it in every part of you and imagine asking for something you need or want. Give yourself time to imagine yourself receiving what you are asking for in this way in every detail. Feel the power and strength in your body, in every part of you, knowing that you fully deserve whatever you are asking for

Homework: Notice this week what feelings you might find most difficult to handle, that might feel overwhelming, or that limit your life in some way.

Week 4 – Handling Feelings Positively

To become more comfortable with our feelings, we need to notice and normalise our feelings in a way that is positive and constructive. We can choose if they help us or hinder us.

CHECK IN: What feelings do you think might be most difficult to handle for you?

ANGER – NEEDS EXPRESSION: Writing down how you feel or even writing letters that you may not send; Assertiveness; Letting off Steam by telling someone how angry you are and why; Exercise or other physical activity to let go of anger; Expressing your anger by painting or drawing it.

SADNESS – NEEDS COMFORT: Talk to a friend; Make yourself a cup of tea or a comforting meal; Ask for a hug from a friend; Watch a relaxing film; Read a favourite book (even a children's book!);

FEAR – NEEDS PROTECTION: Consider how you can keep yourself safe; Get more information; Consider who or what will support you; Create space between yourself and the source of fear; Feel the fear, acknowledge your vulnerability and do it anyway; Take one small step at a time to face your fear.

SHAME, GUILT, SELF-DOUBT – NEEDS TO BE TIME LIMITED: Write what you feel shame or guilt about and write your self-doubt on a piece of paper and eventually, after a time period that feels right to you, decide to destroy it – let it go for good. Distract yourself with something positive and move on.

JEALOUSY AND ENVY – NEEDS TO BE PUT INTO PERSPECTIVE: Envy is useful and can tell us what we want and need in our lives. Jealousy may tell us the strength of our feelings but can be destructive, do something good for yourself instead.

POST-TRAUMATIC STRESS: If you have experienced a seriously traumatic event in your life, you may benefit enormously from seeking professional help to 'debrief' from any trauma. It really can help you to deal with this and release it in a healthy way.

JOY, WHAT MAKES YOU HAPPY AND FULFILLED: Spend time doing things you enjoy. Knowing you are moving in the right direction for yourself. Our default setting can be love, joy, happiness, peace, playfulness, freedom, laughter. It might be a lifelong journey to open ourselves to this.

FORGIVENESS AND COMPASSION GIVES TO US WHEN WE GIVE THIS TO OTHERS – IF AND WHEN WE ARE READY.

Releasing the Trauma of Your Journey

In the group, some of these young men were able to talk about their journey from home to the UK. They gained a lot of support as a group, knowing something of what each of them had been through. It helped them to express their feelings. It was still very hard for them to feel safe, anywhere.

Each young man in this group identified that the feeling they had most needed to contend with was trauma. The trauma of the war in their country which had just been going on for so long. Several young men had lost their fathers, who had died in the war. These young men had lived most days, never knowing if they were going to be taken from their beds in the middle of the night to join the army; the trauma of leaving their homes, their families, in particular their mothers; the trauma of their journey up through Africa, walking through the Sahara desert, living and working in refugee camps on the way. A few of them had earned money for food by burying those refugees who died from starvation, illness and injuries. None of them knew if they would be able to make the journey to Europe, find help, and survive. It helped them to discuss all of this in the group and with each other.

Other options to express feelings: Talking to friends and family; Writing letters (even if you don't send them), writing a journal or diary; Creativity: Writing poetry, painting, drawing, sculpting, modelling clay; Making music, singing, dancing to express feelings; Allow yourself to have a good cry, scream or punch or kick a pillow or cushion, all without hurting yourself or anyone else.

As we mature, we can free ourselves by releasing past attachments, habits and old emotional luggage that we may carry from early childhood. Each of us often carries feelings that can limit us as an adult. Our journey, ideally, is to free ourselves to be the selves we choose to be. We need wisdom, compassion, responsibility and humility to do this. This is what it is to be **HUMAN**. Counselling can help, in many areas of our lives to let go of feelings that are no longer helpful or constructive for you.

Visualisation

Sit comfortably and take deep slow breaths for as long as you need to and feel yourself really relaxing. Imagine any of these feelings we have spoken about that you might most want to be free of. Then imagine, any of these feelings being dissolved with a golden ball of light, full of compassion, lightness and joy. Give yourself the time you need to imagine this process of these feelings being dissolved, your being able to fully let them go. Feel them being replaced by compassion, lightness and joy. Feel the freedom of that exchange.

Homework: Notice any behaviour that has become difficult for you to free yourself from.

Week 5 – Changing Behaviour

Taking action, risking changing something is fundamental to improve our enjoyment and ease of movement in the world. Feel the fear, acknowledge our vulnerability and do it anyway. Act with confidence and grow into it, one small step at a time.

CHECK IN: What old behaviours did you think would be the most difficult for you to let go on?

What Increases Our Motivation to Change?

VALUES: Is whatever you want to achieve or change **IMPORTANT ENOUGH** to change?

ENERGY: Notice who and what gives or takes your energy. If something or someone is right for you, there is usually a positive energy exchange. Is this true for you?

SETTING REALISTIC EXPECTATIONS (Success versus expectations): One step at a time. 70% is better than perfection, because perfection doesn't exist.

KNOWLEDGE, INFORMATION, SELF-AWARENESS, SKILLS AND TRAINING are your friends when you are wanting to achieve or change things for yourself.

BELIEVE YOU DESERVE THIS AND BELIEVE YOU CAN CHANGE.

HOW TO BE FREE: As human beings, our need for change is pitted against our resistance to change. We get used to responding in a certain way. It may be adapted behaviour (being good) or rebellious behaviour (anti-authority). Familiar patterns of behaviour can become comfortable, then habits, then attachments.

***Tell Us*:** What do you think would help you to change?

***Tell Us*:** What has worked in the past to motivate you to make a change or achieve a goal?

***Discuss*:** One small thing that you want to change in this coming week – what would support you from inside you and what would support you from outside you?

***Discuss*:** Each of you could design a stop sign for any behaviour you would like to **STOP**, and a **GO** or an **I CAN** sign for something you would like to do.

Visualisation

Begin this visualisation by sitting in a relaxed way. Take some deep breaths and find a comfortable, steady breathing. Feel your breathing in and breathing out, allow yourself to relax. Imagine sitting in a beautiful and peaceful place. This is your place, where you can go and feel whole, strong and safe, any time you need to relax or recharge. A wise elder, male or female, comes towards you, they sit beside you and they have one strength, skill or capacity that you most need right now. They hand you a box, full of light and in that box is that quality that you particularly need. Imagine breathing in that quality into every part of you. When you are ready, imagine bringing that quality back with you, from this relaxation, for you to use whenever it is needed.

Homework: Commit to change one small thing this week – YOU CAN DO IT!

Additional homework to prepare for the last session. Everyone has the opportunity to give a ten-minute presentation along the lines of: What do each of you value most about your past family life? How do you bring this with you

into this new life? What has been important to you on your journey up to this point? What do each of you miss most from your past? This presentation can be done as individuals, in pairs or in small groups.

Week 6 – Bereavement

CHECK IN: What one thing did you decide to change this week? Discuss in the group, or in pairs.

Valuing Your Past and Bringing It with You

There is such pain in grief and loss but it is a pain that joins all human beings together since universally, most of us experience at some time the loss and grief of losing family, friends, home, country, places, jobs, health, limbs, something that we need, love or value. It is part of our essential human experience to love and to lose. We must give time and respect to the process of grief and the acceptance of the pain of it, within ourselves and within others. There are some things that we can do to make this process easier.

By valuing our past, our homes, our families, our friends, our experiences, we are bringing it with us.

Talk to friends, family, other supporters in our lives.

You can create a shrine to a person or place, where you can put a photograph, something memorable from them, place flowers, light a candle and regularly give time to meditate or just think about what they or it has been to you.

If there is something left unsaid for us, we can write a letter to people to express the unspoken. Obviously, they will not read your letter but in the writing of it, you are expressing something you may need to express. You can also role play reading this letter out to an empty chair and imagine them hearing your words.

You can value the gifts you have received from a person who has been very special in your life. Wrap some empty boxes, large or small, in beautiful paper and you can even write on each box, the gift that you felt you received from them. Keep these in a special place for as long as you need to as an act of respect and love.

You could walk in any nearby accessible labyrinth, meditating on this place or person. I have known people do this and imagine walking the labyrinth with their loved ones and it has been very soothing. You could get support to do this; you don't have to do this on your own.

Two quotes from Ben Furman's Book, "It's Never Too Late to Have a Happy Childhood – From Adversity to Resilience"

"Fortunately, no one owns the future, and that gives us the right to dream and imagine ourselves a happy future. If in your imagination we let the sun shine into our future, its beams will light our present and past as well." (p.82)

> "What is most important, however, is that I have a balance in my life, and an inner wisdom that grows as I live and experience more. My childhood

experiences have brought me lots of wisdom and strength. Even if everything else were taken from me, no one could take away my inner strength and wisdom – quite the contrary".

(last page of the book, from a letter by an unnamed woman who describes her childhood as positive, despite a huge number of horrendous, abusive and traumatic childhood experiences)

Taking Your Space in the Group

Everyone has the opportunity to give a ten-minute presentation on: What do each of you value most about your past family life? How do you bring this with you into this new life? What has been important to you on your journey up to this point? What do each of you miss most from your past? This presentation can be done as individuals, in pairs or in small groups.

In our last session, we talked about bereavement, and I asked them what they missed most about home. Each one of them said they missed their mothers most of all. Fortunately, most of them were able to phone their mothers on Sundays, each week, which was the most important thing for them to do. They were all committed to getting an education here in the UK and doing something positive with their lives.

Visualisation

Body awareness, feel your wholeness; feel yourself taking up the full space of your chair, this room, beyond. Visualise what each of you brings with you into this new life, from your homes and family life. Then, imagine stepping out into the life you would like to have for yourself. Imagine the feeling of getting the support you most need, from yourself, from other people. Imagine living free, to be able to take in love, joy, peace, creativity, wisdom, playfulness, laughter and happiness. What would this look like for you?

It May Be Good to Design a Feedback Form to Give Out to Participants

Or Ask for Feedback as Part of a Discussion

Honouring Your Journey Here

There are times when we are inspired by our clients and simply want to honour them. I felt particularly privileged to work with a remarkable group of young men who had individually escaped from a war-torn country in the Horn of Africa. The poem below was written to describe and honour their extraordinarily difficult journey to the UK. They were amazing to work with and had left their homes when they were between 14 and 16 years old, when soldiers were taking young men of that age from their beds in the middle of the night, to join the army there. It helped me to debrief from the horror of some of their stories and celebrate their courage by writing this poem, which tells the story of many young refugees who escape from wars and make the difficult journey here.

I Had to Leave Eritrea

My father came home, one arm shot away.
His eyes, now struggling to see clearly.
My two elder brothers would never come home.
We knew, now I was 15, soldiers would soon come
and take me by force to fight in this endless war.
It is time to leave my family and the farm I love.

My mother gave me a backpack, drew me a map,
for the beginning of my journey north. I pack my
parent's love, courage, a wallet, a mobile, clothes,
pastries, good coffee from my mother, a water
bottle with a layer of olive oil, to stop evaporation
in the desert, money, my parents can barely afford.

My father hugs me, holds on, I feel his heart beat.
My mother's eyes fill with tears. We hug and hug.
I don't want to let go. I take a deep breath and
walk down to a neighbour's house. He is giving
me a lift to the border, towards the hot, dry desert.
I begin my walk on legs that shake with fear.

I sometimes relive the endless pain and soreness
of my walk. The sun, sand and thirst are my enemies.
I arrive at a massive sprawling camp. I am empty inside.
I am shown a place to rest, to sleep, to eat, to drink.
I am lucky to find people who help me to survive.
I work hard, burying people that were not so fortunate.

I listen, I watch, I learn, I make myself useful.
I long for home, for family, friends, our land.
I plan how to survive and how to move forward.
There are so many stories, some good, some bad.
I ask a lot of questions. I work hard and pray.
I see terrible things that make me cry myself to sleep.

I hear of a safe route out. It means more walking,
using all of my money. It means taking a huge risk.

I get as far as Italy, at last a language, familiar to me.
I work on a farm. I earn money, doing what I love.
I build a good life, first working and then studying.
Eventually, I am able to visit my parents in Eritrea.

In our last session, we talked about bereavement, and I asked them what they missed most about home. Each one of them said they missed their mothers most of all. Fortunately, most of them were able to phone their mothers on Sundays, each week, which was the most important thing for them to do. They were all very committed to getting an education here and doing something positive with their lives.

Case Story of Padma – Breaking Out from Too Much Fear

I decide to walk in the forest on my own today.

I've felt confined inside my garden. Maybe because I was the youngest. I've been fed with family love, music, chatter, games, laughter, books to read and home-cooked meals that remind me of our life before.

There are high expectations of performance from my parents, an older sister who has successfully climbed her ladder as a barrister, an older brother who is in his final year at Cambridge. Generally, my family life is good, but, there is a layer of fear, emanating from each of us, in different ways. We may have survived a bloody war, but having seen people we knew mutilated and killed, those images, that terror, just never go away.

This fear permeates my inner core, causing me to move from relative calm to extreme panic resulting from any stress. It confuses and limits me and is not helped by my mum and dad overprotecting me as the youngest child, which can be infuriating.

I awake this morning and decide that this imprisonment behind our garden gate that I swing on, back and forth, watching the world outside, has to stop.

I'm wearing my new jumper with jeans, I had to fight for, but I decided not to go onto campus today. Instead, I plan to go for a walk in the forest on my own. My mum went off earlier to visit Nani. I hide my college bag in my wardrobe. I pack a water bottle, humus and chutney sandwiches and a packet of crisps into a small rucksack. I swap my shoes for walking boots and socks I've hardly ever worn. I walk into the centre of town and wait for a bus. My heart is racing. After a short drive through town, we are out into the countryside which looks bigger today against the blue sky. I sit tight with tension in case I miss my bus stop. I feel heavy as I climb off the bus.

I walk down the long winding lane into the forest. I walk through the largely empty car park and head off on one of the walks. My head hurts with the possibilities of bad things that can happen to me in the woods. I feel stupid not to have brought my phone with me. I realised as I was leaving home that it needed charging. That would have made me feel safer, I never go anywhere without it. My mouth is dry. My body is trembling.

My steps are hesitant as I follow a vaguely familiar path, there is no one else around. I have been here with my father before but it feels very different today. My heart is thumping, so I take some deep breaths and walk faster. Everything in me is screaming, 'stop', 'go home' as I get deeper into the forest. I decide to walk faster. I find a rhythm and gradually begin to look around.

A small stream vanishes into nothing, leaving dry cracked earth. It is a dry autumn. So many of the leaves have fallen early, covering the forest floor. Thorns at the side of the path hold a tiny white feather captive. This oddly reassures me as a 'sign' that I'm doing the right thing. I look up and see sunbeams escaping from a cloud sliding down to undo four petal heads of a dying yellow flower, a left over from summer. I want to sketch it when I get home. My shakiness is slowing, and my legs feel stronger. I begin to enjoy the feel of walking on the hard, dry earth and the earthy smell of the forest. I feel my whole body move as one. The sky is a polished blue. I stop and breathe in the beauty of the trees all around me. A feisty blackbird complains about being disturbed. I realise that my whole body is smiling. I've forgotten how good it is simply to walk out, swing my arms, find a pace that feels comfortable. The thought of sitting inside a stuffy lecture theatre, even listening to something I'm really interested in, seems weird to me today. Here I feel free, in a world that fills my senses.

I find a tall Wellingtonia that I used to love to hug. It stands much taller than the trees around it. I throw down my rucksack and jump over a ditch to get to it. I stretch my arms around the tree as far as I can reach, face pressed up against the bark. It is softer than I remember. I'm sure I can feel a deep pulse. It feels like a sister, tall and singing with life. I hold on gently, not wanting to damage the bark, not wanting to let go. I feel its strength. We are both growing. I drag myself away, all panic gone.

I jump back over the ditch, pick up my rucksack and walk on. I notice the sun highlight a spider's web, spun in between two branches of a pine tree; it looks so fragile. How do they do that?

I find a huge neatly rounded anthill with not one ant in sight. I remember being inspired to see how they work together. Maybe there is a lesson here for us as human beings, if only we could co-operate, rather than fight and kill each other, think what we could achieve. I hated how fiercely competitive some people were at school, coming up to 'A' levels. It put so much pressure on all of us, even teachers who were normally great, were just more bad-tempered and stressed. At least art college doesn't feel so pressurised, yet!

I decide it's time to head back. I notice the patterns made on the path by the shadows of nettles, ferns and holly. Maybe I could use these in my end-of-term art project, I wish I had my phone to take some pictures. I can't stop smiling. The joy of this funfair of nature has devoured my fear. I don't think I realised before how deep and for how long the fear of our old life infiltrated every part of me. I can't really remember feeling safe in my body, free to explore the world around me. I grew up with a deep sense of my parents' fear for me, my brother and sister, it has never really gone away, despite the fact that we have made a good life here for the past four years. Those memories, that feeling of being suddenly out of control, in danger at any moment. It's still there, in every one of us, in different ways.

I'm glad I decided to seek out some counselling at college. I wouldn't have dared do this walk today without it. This has turned into a good 'home-work' for me to choose to do and write about as part of my counselling. I feel as if I have reclaimed back something of my real self today.

Part 4

The Effects on Us, Working as a Counsellor

Debriefing

I found, early on in my life as a university counsellor, that I was in absolute awe of the capacity of clients, not only to survive but to develop successful loving relationships when they may not have experienced even the most basic kindness in their young lives. These more extreme life histories can be very difficult to hear, especially when we begin this work. The gift of trust that our clients give us is humbling when sharing their challenging experiences and innermost feelings, some never spoken about before and yet readily shared in the counselling with a disarming honesty.

I watch on the news the amazing work of the International Federation of the Red Cross & the Red Crescent (IFRC), who put themselves in grave danger physically to help rescue people on both sides of any conflict in the world. As therapists, we don't normally place ourselves in physical danger, but there was something I recognised in the humility and love that these people expressed about their work that was familiar to me. Therapists and counsellors are sometimes faced with children and adults who have experienced terrible situations in their lives, and it is impossible not to be deeply affected by both the disturbing nature of some clients' experiences and by the courage and indomitable spirit that many of our clients have had, in order to survive such experiences.

When we truly listen to another person, who is courageous enough to be honest and share their deepest feelings and thoughts, it involves every part of us, body, heart, mind, soul and spirit. It is that intimacy where real work can be done, but it also needs to be protected by strong boundaries on both sides, not just in terms of time and place but also in terms of confidentiality and respect for both client and counsellor, the awareness of taking care of ourselves once the counselling session or the counselling day ends. It is important to acknowledge this for our clients and for ourselves.

For counsellors to be most effective and keep ourselves emotionally and psychologically safe, individual and group supervision is essential and very much a part of the normal ethics and practice of most counsellors and therapists. Case supervision with an external supervisor and with colleagues, especially in a university, college

DOI: 10.4324/9781003754244-24

or school setting is an invaluable support to the work that we are doing. It is also important to have a sufficient level of ongoing support and continuous training to update and refresh our skills, motivation and contact with colleagues both in our own institutions and nationally, to encourage best practice.

It is vital for each of us as counsellors to find the best ways for us to debrief from, the most difficult to hear, histories of our clients. Working in a university setting with international students, I found I occasionally worked with clients who had been soldiers and victims of war. It is extremely difficult to hear stories of extreme violence and war and what it does to ordinary people and families. Debriefing is vital, not only with colleagues in group supervision or in individual supervision, but we also need to recognise and take care of our needs on a daily and weekly basis. On our campus, we have a beautiful York stone-built labyrinth, and a walk in this labyrinth, over-looking as it does a grassy hill and a view of Canterbury Cathedral, was a wonderful way of debriefing. Also, for me writing was sometimes an important way of expressing my feelings, bearing in mind the importance of confidentiality. Sometimes, we just need to spend time with friends and family and do something joyful, which enables us to switch off and relax. For many of us, it is good to have children and pets to play with, lovely countryside to walk in and an active social life with good friends. I also found it useful to do yoga and meditation and to have regular cranial sacral therapy treatments. Although our work is supported by group and individual supervision, it is very important for us to find many different ways to let go of the distress that often faces us in the counselling room.

Sometimes, what I found hardest of all was the frustration and impotence of listening to clients' experiences, repeated again and again, of childhood sexual abuse and rape of children, mainly men, but occasionally women who would never be reported to the police and never go to court. This is because there was no trust or confidence in most of our clients that victims would be treated well, that they would be believed and that the perpetrators would be punished. Hardly anyone that I worked with, over a period of 35 plus years, had reported their rape or abuse to the police. This means that we, as a world, probably have absolutely no idea just how prevalent such crimes really are. The figures that are collected are a complete underestimation of such crimes.

In our counselling service, we had met the police women who dealt with rape victims and had visited the police safe house, but despite any of our reassurances to clients about explaining that there are good people there to help and support them, the vast majority of clients didn't trust the court system or the police, to bring a conviction and, most of all, they didn't want to ever face the perpetrator again. Our system of law simply doesn't inspire trust in our legal system to protect such victims from what might feel like 'further abuse' to them.

Working in a university city, it became obvious, especially in the first term of new students arriving, that there were 'rape operators' who preyed on vulnerable new students, who had been used to having parties and sleepovers in their hometowns and knowing everyone. They arrived on campus having mostly experienced being safe with people they had grown up with. The first term of university, each year, unfortunately, brought several young freshers to the counselling service, having been raped. This crime is still not being treated in a way that stops it from happening again and again. It is very upsetting for us as counsellors to realise that society does not yet take this crime seriously enough.

Fresh Meat

Smart, beautiful, loved.
You arrive on campus, innocent.
I hear your pain.
You would have been safe at home staying at the party house,
having three glasses of wine, because you knew everyone.
This is a different place.
You're a fresher.
He's an operator,
preying on new students.
You clearly said, *'no'*.
He hurt you badly.
I hear that you don't want to report him,
don't want to repeat the whole experience, in police hands,
in a court where you will be judged, where his history won't be told.
I'm sorry that this has happened to you.
I'm sorry that this happens every year,
to young women fresh from home, where you knew everyone.
I'm sorry that the law doesn't always protect young women from rape.

Working with many survivors of sexual abuse and rape as children and as adults can be extremely disturbing. At times, we may all need some extra self-care, and it is important to have an awareness of when this is necessary and to think about what would be most beneficial for ourselves in this situation. Again, thank goodness for group and individual supervision, which is such a wonderful support in this work. I always found that writing poetry, singing in a choir, walking in the countryside, meditation, yoga, occasional massages and cranial sacral therapy kept me in balance. It is important for each of us to think about what most recharges and revitalises us while doing this work.

Taking It Home

One of the gifts of working as a counsellor is the excitement of exploring 'how we develop'. I enjoyed the 'detective work', as we become more aware of our own story in our training and begin to make sense of that, before moving on to insights and awareness of the people we are working with. Counselling helps us to identify what beliefs, decisions and defences operated in our own families and in ourselves to produce certain patterns of behaviour, thinking and feelings that we may repeat consciously or unconsciously, even when it may have obvious negative outcomes.

In our own supervision and counselling, we are all given space to consider what we want to happen in the future. These 'ah-ha' moments can then free us to make different choices or to accept existing choices that we have become comfortable with.

As counsellors, this exploration of human behaviour, in all its multilayered variations, continues in our own lives, whether we want it to or not. The awareness that we gain about ourselves and the people around us is hard to 'switch off'. It can be exciting, humbling, annoying and scary as we hone our skills and intuition to a high degree. It is understandable that people close to us might be threatened by being seen as a specimen under a microscope, especially when we are training! Counsellors in training can often be guilty of this.

My first somewhat unwilling client was certainly my husband. I learnt, early on, to rein in my enthusiastic 'detective' and realised that 'a little knowledge can be a dangerous thing'.

Fortunately, we do learn to handle the knowledge and power we amass as we grow in our understanding of human behaviour. I often guess what is going to happen in a drama rather too quickly because of that highly tuned awareness that we gradually develop in doing this work. Sometimes, we see things that we may not want to see in people. When working as a counsellor, creating strong boundaries for ourselves is a very necessary protection for us, for our clients, for our friends and family.

I began to question a world that sometimes seems to require us to be 'perfect' and how impossible and troublesome this can be. How much easier our lives become when we allow ourselves gratitude for what we have and do, and when we decide to accept, with grace, being the best we can be. I used to keep a sign on my noticeboard, **'70%'**, as something to aim for. After all, if the muscles in our body are stretched 70%, it is healthy, but if pushed too far, they can be strained. Aiming for perfection, which is a bizarre expectation in our world, is not only impossible but can lead to dissatisfaction, pressure and sometimes a rebellious procrastination.

AI Counsellors?

This brings me to the idea of AI counsellors or chatbots. AI chatbots are already being used to provide initial support and triage advice, helping individuals determine if they need further mental health care. AI tools could possibly be used to practice new skills. AI chatbots can provide support between therapy/counselling sessions if a counsellor is unavailable, perhaps to give some level of reassurance. AI chatbots can provide 24/7 access to a basic level of support, which could be helpful for people unable to access traditional mental health care. They can provide a safe and anonymous space for individuals to talk about their feelings and challenges if there is a lack of human contact or social isolation. However, what is missing in any contact with an AI is human emotional intelligence and the power of human intuition and compassion. There may also be difficulties with ethical concerns and bias. This makes for an interesting discussion as the world of AI evolves.

The Power of Counselling

The hope is that we are able to provide a safe place for our clients, which enables self-expression and self-awareness to blossom into self-realisation. We can all misuse our power by wanting to have power 'over' others. It is important, as counsellors, for us to encourage our clients to own their power, to do, to be and to have. It is important that we need to be able to let go, be ourselves and be present with our clients in their process. When we let go, something magical seems to happen in our clients. In this safe space that we help to create, perhaps we become a catalyst to a rather more unexplained, spiritual aspect to the counselling process, enabling our clients to tap into a universal source of energy and understanding. This can be powerful and ordinary at the same time. This quote by Diane Mariechild, (**5**) seems to describe this:

> The dominant culture views power as power over another person, another group, another culture. Power is expressed as aggression...This kind of power creates enormous pain and suffering. True power, is subtle. It is an alignment, a harmony with all of life. It is connected to and working for the good of all life. It is impersonal. It has no preference. This power to connect is magical and at the same time absolutely ordinary. It is awakening to life. To love, and to know that you are loving, this is power.

Humour and play can be very powerful in the counselling process. Walking through the University Counselling service that I worked in, it was quite common to hear laughter coming from the rooms.

It is part of our work to help clients to identify their repeat patterns, and humour is sometimes inevitable.

Often if a client referred to themselves as '*stupid*', I would gently challenge them each time until this became something we could both laugh at. There is something valuable in being able to laugh at what we do that normalises it as something we all do 'sometimes'. It is an essential part of being human.

It can be hard for us, as counsellors, to adjust back to ordinary life from the 'rarefied' atmosphere in the counselling room, in supervision and in case discussions where there is a high level of awareness, honesty, vulnerability and intimacy. It can be difficult to adjust to social situations in the outside world, where some relationships can seem more superficial. On the other hand, it has made me seek out people and groups that are more aware, intimate and open about sharing vulnerability and most of all people who have a sense of humour!

Our ability to actively listen may need to be managed. Sometimes, when I've been in a workshop, I've noticed that a speaker may more often seem to talk to me, and I manage this sometimes by looking away.

Also, this skill can occasionally elicit intimate confidences from people, in social situations, that we may not want to be in receipt of. It is important to be aware of how powerful our skills can become. We can also get used to feeling responsible for other people, and it is important for us, as counsellors, to be responsible for protecting our own boundaries as well as the boundaries of other people.

Blind Spots

There are times when a client's story will resonate with our own experiences, and for us to do this work effectively, it is vital that we have access to and the will to seek therapy for ourselves when necessary.

Our work benefits us enormously because we are required to have individual supervision, case discussions and ongoing professional development. Without this, we can all develop 'blind spots'. I rarely worked with a child abuser, but on one occasion, early on in my counselling career, I worked with a man who had been a convicted paedophile. He had almost managed to convince me that 'he hadn't **really** abused the children that he had been sent to prison for abusing'. I got short shrift from my colleagues and supervisor when I presented him at the next case discussion. As a result, I was more challenging of his beliefs, and the work with him moved forward much more positively and realistically.

Another blind spot for me was a time when I was simply doing too much. I was taking a Shepherd's Pie out of the oven at home and the tea-towel slipped from my hand. I dropped it, managed to guide it to the floor safely, but the boiling potato bounced out of the pot onto my bare left foot.

I was left with a serious burn and had to take a month off from work. Too late, I realised that I was 'burnt out'. I am sure this 'accident' happened because I was not taking sufficient care of my own needs.

Leaving Us with Bigger Questions

I visited a beautiful cathedral in Budapest with two friends. We went into the cathedral and decided to do a meditation in this beautiful place. I looked up at the beautiful golden dome and the exquisite paintings, some depicting soldiers dressed in armour, going to war, carrying swords and killing people and others depicting daily life, full of love, beauty and laughter.

At home, I'd been working with a female client who had been violently raped by two men. I lit a candle at one of the altar pieces and sat with the question: Why is there so much violence and abuse in the world?

The answer came to me and of course, it was obvious. Just as there is day and night, hot and cold, so there is love and creativity on a continuum with cruelty and destructiveness.

We mostly have a free choice; sometimes people will choose creativity and sometimes cruelty and very often, somewhere in between. I believe, most of us do the best we can, loving our families and friends, wanting the best for them and others. It is a relatively low percentage of people who go on to do something truly awful or are completely indifferent to the plight of others.

When we listen to the nightly news, there is inevitably more coverage of negative or violent incidents.

Is this because it is more dramatic? There is certainly more coverage of the people in positions of power who are just making bad choices with wars, violence, entitlement and extreme ego and narcissism.

But when we look around at the people we know personally, family, friends, work colleagues, clients, people at large, they seem mostly good and often wonderful.

It can help us in our work to find support in a philosophy, a spiritual belief or a spiritual practice. I have consistently found teachers and inspiration in colleagues, supervisors, writers, philosophers, some films, artists and most of all in family and friends, coming together to support each other. Perhaps, most of all,

I feel great hope in watching children and now grandchildren, growing up into really good people.

In my work as Head of a University Counselling Service, I have seen so many clients really change their lives around in the most positive ways. It makes our work incredibly satisfying and makes me feel optimistic about the real world that we live in. I just know the world is mostly full of good people who mostly make good choices for themselves and others.

Part 5

Ethical Frameworks

Ethical Frameworks

Because of the confidential and personal nature of the work of therapy and counselling, working as a counsellor, therapist or psychotherapist requires that we are guided in our codes of practice by a strong professional ethical framework. The British Association of Counsellors and Psychotherapy (BACP), which was founded in 1977, has such a professional ethical framework. This is the professional body of which I became a member in the 1980s, eventually becoming accredited with BACP as a senior accredited registered practitioner in 1993, 1999, 2004 and then annually for many years until retirement. For many years I was also accredited with the Association for University and College Counsellors.

When you become a member of such a professional body you commit to comply with their ethical framework, which is the main point of reference for any professional conduct hearings. It is very important to familiarise yourself with the ethical framework of whatever professional body you decide to join. Such ethical frameworks are there to protect us as counsellors and therapists and our clients. BACP has three main sections: "A commitment to clients provides a summary of working to professional standards and building an ethical relationship; Ethics specifies the values, principles and personal moral qualifies that inform our work and underpin supervision; Good practice considers the application of our commitments to clients and ethics to our practice".

Although members of such a professional body join voluntarily, most employers, such as universities, would expect that the counsellor that they employ would be members of an ethical body such as BACP. Such a body requires a code of ethics, which is vital to the work of counsellors and therapists. In the case of this code of ethics at BACP, this includes high standards of both ethics and good practice. According to BACP, "ethical bodies have three main functions: to provide information on counselling and psychotherapy services and set standards which give the general public a route to complain if they feel dissatisfied with the service they have received from a counsellor; if the complaint is upheld then a counsellor or therapist can find themselves receiving a 'sanction'".

DOI: 10.4324/9781003754244-25

BACP states that such a sanction could be: "a directive to undertake more training, submit a report to an ethical committee, explaining how they have altered their practice so the same problem doesn't arise again".

BACP also state that: "In extreme cases, a counsellor can be 'struck off' which means their membership of the organization, is terminated".

BACP also states that: "Ethical bodies also provide support to counsellors and psychotherapists in the form of well-researched information, continued professional development, training courses, and a collective voice when dealing with the government of the day and any legislation they propose".

It is important to inform yourself as a counsellor of the procedures of the BACP, most of which you can find on the BACP website, especially as they also set the requirements and limits of confidentiality. This is such an important part of the trust in the relationship between the counsellor and our clients. There are other ethical bodies that issue codes of practice in Counselling and Psychotherapy in the UK, and there is a list on the BACP website. There is also mention there of possible conflicts when counsellors are working with two ethical codes of practice.

It is important when we begin working with clients that we let them know what code of ethics we work to and indeed give them assurances of our confidentiality guidelines.

Working on a university campus, it is essential that we have appropriate supervision, if possible individual supervision and group supervision within the counselling service itself. This is an important part of keeping ourselves and our clients safe. The guidance and experience that is contained in such a group and in our supervision enables us to be the best counsellors we can be.

Where possible it is helpful to meet with other student support staff on campus and particularly nurture good contacts with the university medical centre. Each university is different in what they can offer but it is in the interest of the students and the counselling staff, especially trainee counsellors, to have good social networks amongst the many different student services.

Part 6

Professional Support for Counsellors

Choosing a Placement and a Supervisor

An important way to find eventual employment is through the experience and networking one achieves during a placement. Therefore, it would be beneficial to choose a placement in an area of work that interests you. Consider the various contexts in which you might choose to work (Education, H.E. F.E. Special Needs Teaching; Primary Care; Religious/Spiritual; Prison/Probation; Relate; Employment; Media; Youth Work; Private practice; etc.). If you eventually want to set up in private practice, where might you find the widest possible experience in a placement? What do you, as a trainee, want from a placement and a placement supervisor? Do you want a supervisor who works in a similar or in a complementary way? Negotiate a suitable contract with your supervisor and ask yourself whether you will be able to work comfortably and confidently in this setting with this person. Will the clients you would be seeing count towards accreditation? Will you need your own Insurance? And most important of all: Will you be safe? (panic buttons, people around etc.).

Boundaries and Contracts

As you grow in experience, and if the service you are working with is building up a long waiting list, you might like to experiment contracting with the client in different ways of working. You might have some clients you could work with in a single session, weekly, monthly, fortnightly or even using monthly check-ins. It is vital to manage safe and secure boundaries with the client, and this is something that is useful to discuss in your supervision. How will you manage a request from a client who wants to see you outside of the counselling? How much self-disclosure is too much? These are helpful things to discuss in your supervision or group supervision. It is helpful to review, in your supervision, the focus and the contract regularly if you are doing longer-term counselling. It is important to keep a balance between challenge and support. Notice whether the client is a 'visitor', 'complainant' or 'client'. Group supervision is an invaluable help for discussions on many of these topics.

DOI: 10.4324/9781003754244-26

Other Practical and Alternative Supports

It is helpful for the counselling service to have handouts for clients on a variety of subjects but also including meditations, visualisations and relaxations. It is also important to have knowledge of and regular contact with the other student and staff services offered on campus, such as the Medical Centre, Learning Support, Disability Support, the Chaplaincy, Health and Safety, Personnel Department and the Sports Centre, which may offer various exercise or yoga classes. It would be important to keep a list of local alternative therapeutic support also, e.g. Reflexology, Shiatsu, Massage, Bach flower remedies, Cranial Sacral Therapy, Kinesiology, Nutrition Advice and any others available. Even learning to drive might benefit some clients. It is helpful for us as counsellors to have suitable contact, awareness and information of as many other agencies as possible that can offer support to students.

Bringing Case Notes Alive

It is most important to bear in mind the most recent legal requirements for case notes and the implications of any current revisions to the Data Protection Act. It is essential to discuss this with your supervisor, living as we do in an ever-increasing litigious society and compensation culture.

When you begin counselling, there is the dynamism of a counselling session, working as you are in the present with what the clients bring, often a challenging and unpredictable process. After that enlivening process, it can feel laborious to have to write case notes; it can even feel as if they are a dead weight. Are they an aid to recalling the client's history, or are they a safeguard in case of litigation? How can you bring that process alive?

I searched for a way of bringing case notes alive for me. I was delighted to discover several ideas that have gone on to enhance the process of counselling and supervision. It is good if we can find our own way of working and our own creative style for producing a record of our counselling sessions.

Firstly, you can make them shorter and less verbatim. You could summarise them, it might help you to learn something about the essence of each client session, awareness about what is most important about each session, insights into the process of the counselling itself and what actually went on in the session.

If it appeals to you, you could sometimes draw a colourful diagram to represent each client, their relationship and the issues in their lives. I found it interesting to draw a large picture with the initial of the client's first name or a shape that represented them in some way. Each diagram evolved as I focussed on that client and their process and added shapes and colours that represented something about them, people and relationships around them and their process. Each session brought more insights. This was fun to do and just occasionally I would show it to the client and ask for their feedback, explaining what the different shapes had represented from our session. They would often add ideas themselves, which was very creative.

It was valuable to present these pictures/diagrams/drawings in supervision as I gained insights from my intuitive choice of colours and positioning of character or aspects in the client's life. This led on to an innovative way of presenting clients at Supervision when I might have felt a bit swamped and needed an overview of my whole client load. I would sometimes draw a coloured landscape, roughly drawn, as I am certainly not an artist. This could include mountains, lakes, rough patches of quicksand, shale or even bunkers! A wide path could sometimes meander through the picture, and I would place on the whole picture each client in my case load and where I felt they were on their path through their counselling, some at the beginning, some reflecting in lakes, some stuck in muddy bunkers, which may have been more about me than the clients!

Just occasionally, I might involve the client and use the immediacy of the session itself to ask clients if they would spend the last five minutes of each session helping me to record a summary of the session. This worked really well. Clients would often enjoy a time to review and reflect on the session, and I would write down salient points and issues that both of us remembered and wanted to highlight and record. I discovered that some clients felt included and enjoyed the mutuality of responsibility for this process, and some clients appreciated their words being remembered and recorded, especially clients who had past experiences of not being listened to.

The next step in this journey stemmed from two changes. Firstly, in doing more supervision myself, I became used to writing notes on supervisee's clients during each supervision session. Secondly, we changed the format of our assessments so that we not only recorded more history from the client at assessment but also spent more time helping the client discover a focus for their prospective counselling. In doing this, I became adept at using a clipboard, completing a lengthy form and the ability to maintain a level of eye contact, interest and connection, which enabled each client to feel properly met and listened to.

This all led to finding different ways of recording case notes that made the whole process come alive. Sometimes, I would use the clipboard and a blank sheet of paper through the counselling sessions themselves as part of the communication with the client. I used the taking of notes as a dynamic tool, underlining or circling certain words and phrases which the client used repeatedly or which seemed particularly important and highlighting issues and relationships that they felt were most relevant to them. I found myself drawing diagrams and using the clipboard as a blackboard to reflect something back to the client or to highlight a piece of theory with the client, even stopping the client and asking them to elaborate on something and emphasising its importance by writing it down and repeating it out loud. Just as there is a choice in the questions we ask clients, so there is an additional choice about what warrants being written down and summarised.

What is also important is that there were often times, it felt important to stop this process entirely and give absolute attention to what the client was saying or feeling. I did not use this process in every session or with every client; it was simply an option which, for various reasons, could be valuable. I certainly would not have considered doing this when the client is sharing distressing or painful feelings. I also would not consider doing this with new clients in a first session.

At times, using the clipboard was like having a third person in the room, and indeed there is an additional relationship in the counselling room to be managed, which I found an exciting challenge. An added bonus for me is that I felt more energised in being able to shift my body and eye focus.

Over and above the ways of recording case notes I have described, I recognise that it is important to write Supervision Notes about our own feelings and process, these too could be done in a creative way. I encourage all counsellors to find their own way of recording notes and using them, if appropriate, in counselling or supervision.

It is most important to bear in mind the most recent legal implications of case notes and the implications of any current revisions to the Data Protection Act. It is essential to discuss this with your supervisor, living as we do in an ever-increasing litigious society and compensation culture.

Beginning Your Paid Work as a Counsellor

When seeking paid counselling work, it is important to think about what kind of work might most appeal to you: working for an agency or becoming self-employed. Working in any particular setting or environment. In a medical setting, an educational setting or a work setting. It is good to network with other counsellors, get as much information as you can, even test out some part-time placements to widen your experience. Talk to other counsellors who have begun in private practice to find out whether that appeals to you, given sufficient experience first. Do you want to do full-time or part-time work to begin with? Do you want to work in the daytime or in the evenings?

If your anxiety level is high, you could organise a supervision before you begin and discuss things that might lessen your anxiety. Normalising the anxiety of beginning and realising that you have much to offer just by listening and 'being there' for your client. Has the client been assessed? Do you want to check the assessment notes first or see the client through your own eyes first? Will very distressed clients be filtered out at first? Fears about a suicidal client? How many clients do you feel comfortable beginning with? What do you need from the client in order to work with them? Contracts, confidentiality guidelines, contact with the client – meet with the receptionist/secretary and find out how it all works, especially the forms and statistics. Take it one step at a time and don't expect to know how it all works right now!

It is vital that high on the list of priorities of any counsellor or therapist is protection and support. First the use of supervision: what do you most want from each session? (you could make a contract at the beginning). It can be about you too, if there is something going on for you that is draining, traumatic or difficult (aside from the fact that you are doing or have recently finished a therapy or counselling training!), it is important to let your supervisor know. What impacts on you impact your work, and it is important that you get support. Useful areas of discussion are boundary issues, client work where you feel stuck or just need a lift to help move the client on and do share the aspects where you are doing really well. Find out what happens if your supervisor is away or if you need to talk to your supervisor urgently!

All counsellors and therapists have a responsibility to protect themselves where they work, in the form of a 'panic button' or having other people around while they are working, especially if they have concerns about a client. Also, ensure that you know what confidentiality guidelines are in operation and what ethics and guidelines for good practice are adhered to in your placement.

Your Counselling Room

You may have your own counselling room/office. You may have to share your room with other counsellors, but do give some time and effort to make it comfortable for you. You will be spending many hours in this room. Can you reflect the protection, comfort and self-expression which we hope to promote in our clients. What do you want your room to say or not to say? It is an important space and needs to create an atmosphere and feeling that you most need around you in order to do this work.

Professional and Personal Development

Choosing your professional body and utilising their professional ethics and guidelines is vital in doing this work. It is positive to begin working towards accreditation. Choosing how you keep records and statistics of your clients. Keeping up with professional development and ongoing training.

It is important to commit to work towards becoming a professional and authentic counsellor and to continue your own life journey in whatever way is right for you. You need to decide your own path and career development, to keep yourself in balance and continue your personal development, wherever it is needed most. It is important for you to stay aware of your own needs to develop emotionally, intellectually, physically, creatively, spiritually and even playfully!

Learning from Your Clients

It is helpful to work from the assumption that your client is the expert on themselves. How did the client approach the counselling? How do they enter the room? How do they appear, sit and relate to you? What is their body telling you and them? Where is their energy as they tell you about themselves? What is going on in their lives right now? Where have they come from? Consider the patterns of birth and early life, their position in their family. How might this be influencing them now? How do they invite you to feel?

What does the client give most to other people? It might be what they most need. What is the prime relationship like with themselves? What do they need in order to feel whole? What are their experiences of the culture they have grown up in, and how does it feel that you may have grown up in a different culture from them? Enjoy the process of honing your skills of listening, noticing and connecting.

If a client is feeling unable to access their inner feelings or thoughts, it can be useful to ask them to find other ways of expressing themselves, such as a visualisation, a drawing or a role play. It could be an expression of something from the past, present or a concern or feeling about the future. Most people know, somewhere in themselves, more than they may realise. It is useful to find different ways to help our clients access their feelings, blocks and beliefs. It may be that they can more easily draw or describe where they want to be in the future and consider what steps they need to take to get to that place and what might be blocking them.

If the client is 'stuck' or 'blocked' in some way, you can always ask them about 'stories, films, songs that they may identify with. If they feel stuck in their thinking or feelings, they might be able to identify feeling something in their bodies. There are many paths to increasing our self-awareness.

Sometimes our clients feel out of balance in some way, we can ask them what might they think or feel would bring them back into balance. Many people are intuitive about what is really going on inside them, but they might need prompts from us, as counsellors.

What behaviour, thoughts, feelings, does the client want to change, leave behind, welcome in? Feelings mostly tell us what we need, sadness may need comfort: fear may need protection, anger may need a safe form of expression, and joy often needs sharing.

Homework can be helpful as a way of increasing the emphasis on what they do in the week in-between; keeping a journal; getting in touch with their own creativity; asking for support or comfort; finding safe expressions of feelings; the place of ritual in bereavement, and letting go.

Referrals

Seek advice from your supervisor but it is vital that you have good information about the availability of appropriate emergency services, local psychiatric and medical services, both on campus and in the locality. There would be some discussion here of appropriate consultation and confidentiality issues. What supports, specialist or differing types of therapy and groupwork exist on campus and in your local area? You can discuss with your supervisor and in any group supervision what circumstances might point to the need for a referral and how best you would discuss this with your clients.

It is also important to have knowledge and contact with the other student and staff services offered on campus, such as the Medical Centre, Learning Support, Disability Support, the Chaplaincy, Health and Safety, Personnel Department, the Sports Centre, which may offer various exercise or yoga classes. It would be important to keep a list of local alternative therapeutic support also, e.g. Reflexology, Shiatsu, Massage, Bach flower remedies, Cranial Sacral Therapy, Kinesiology, Nutrition Advice, and any others available. Even learning to drive might benefit some clients. It is helpful for us as counsellors to have suitable contact, awareness and information of as many other agencies that can offer support to students as possible.

Book List for Counsellors and Clients

A Clinician's Guide to Neurodiversity; 2025, Routledge, by Sarah Ashworth-Watts

Anti-Discrimination Practice in Counselling and Psychotherapy; 2010, Sage Publishing, by Colin Lago

Counselling Skills in Action; 2020, Sage Publishing, by Tim Bond and Megan Rose Stafford

Creativity in Counselling Children and Adolescents; 2023, Routledge, by Teresa Behrend Fletcher and Amanda C. DeDiego

Essentials of Compassion Focused Therapy, A Practical Manual for Clinicians; 2024, Routledge, by Nicola Petrocchi, James Kirby, Beatrice Baldi

Everyday Zen; 1977, Harper Collins by Charlotte Joko Beck.

Feel the Fear and Do It Anyway; 1987, Penguin Classics, by Susan Jeffers.

Finding Love in the Looking Glass: A Book of Counselling Case Stories; 2014, Routledge, by Maggie Yaxley Smith.

Inside Counselling: Becoming and Being a Professional Counsellor; 1997, Sage Publishing, by Anthony Crouch

Intersections of Privilege & Otherness in Counselling & Psychotherapy; 2021, Routledge, by Dwight Turner

It's Never Too Late to Have a Happy Childhood: From Adversity to Resilience; 1998, BT Press, by Ben Furman.

Learning with the Labyrinth: Creating Reflective Space in Higher Education; 2016, Edited by Jan Sellers & Bernard Moss

Letters to a Young Therapist; 2016, Basic Books, by Mary Bray Pipher

More Than Miracles; 2007, Routledge, by Steve de Shazer

Neurodiversity-Affirming Psychotherapy, Clinical Pathways to Autistic Mental Health; 2024, Routledge, by Ruth Strunz

Open Mind: Women's Daily Inspiration for Becoming Mindful; 1995 HarperOne, by Diane Mariechild

Person Centred Counselling in Action; 2013, Sage Publishing, by Dave Mearns and Brian Thorne

Person Centred Therapy Today; 2000, Sage Publishing, by Dave Mearns and Brian Thorne

Radical Relational Perspectives in Transactional Analysis Psychotherapy; 2024, Routledge, by Karen Minikin

So You Want to Do Narrative Therapy? Letters to an Inspiring Narrative Therapist; 2024, Routledge, by Sanni Paljakka, Tom Stone Carlson and Epton David (Foreword)

The Art of Happiness; 1999, Hodder Paperbacks, by 14th Dalai Lama & Howard C. Cutler

The Future: Ring the Bells That Still Can Ring; 1992, Anthem Lyrics from Album by Leonard Cohen.

The Handbook of Music Therapy; 2024, Routledge, by Leslie Bunt, Sarah Hoskyns & Sangeeta Swamy

The Pain We Carry: Healing from Complex PTSD for People of Colour; 2022, New Harbinger Publications, by Natalie Y. Gutierrez

The Power of Now: A Guide to Spiritual Enlightenment; 2001, Hodder & Stoughton, by Eckhart Tolle

Therapy The Basics; 2025, Routledge, by Sissy Iykou

The Resilient Practitioner Burnout and Compassion Fatigue Prevention and Self Care Strategies for the Helping Professions; 2024, Routledge, by Thomas M. Skovholt and Michelle Trotter-Mathison

The Subtle Spectrum: An Honest Account of Autistic Discovery, Relationships & Identity; 2021, Routledge, by Joanna Grace

What It Is to Be Transgender: Video on Philosophy Tube (800,000 Followers), 77, by Abigail Thorn.

Bibliography

Beck, Charlotte Joko. *Everyday Zen*, 76. Harper/Collins, 1977.

Cohen, Leonard. "The Future," *Ring the Bells That Still Can Ring*, 76. Anthem Lyrics from Album, 1992.

Furman, Ben. *It's Never Too Late to Have a Happy Childhood: From Adversity to Resilience*, 112. BT Press, 1998.

Jeffers, Susan. *Feel the Fear and Do It Anyway*, 87. Penguin Classics, 1987.

Mariechild, Diane. *Open Mind: Women's Daily Inspiration for Becoming Mindful*, 119. HarperOne, 1995.

Thorn, Abigail. What It Is to Be Transgender: Video on Philosophy Tube (800,000 Followers), 77.

For Product Safety Concerns and Information please contact our EU
representative GPSR@taylorandfrancis.com
Taylor & Francis Verlag GmbH, Kaufingerstraße 24, 80331 München, Germany

www.ingramcontent.com/pod-product-compliance
Ingram Content Group UK Ltd.
Pitfield, Milton Keynes, MK11 3LW, UK
UKHW020003200926
475702UK00015B/2445
* 9 7 8 1 0 4 1 2 7 4 1 2 4 *